CONTENTS

1
Introducing Berlin

Berlin, the once divided city at the heart of Europe, now restored as the political capital of a united German nation, never ceases to fascinate and amaze. As the seat of the Hohenzollern dynasty, the hotbed of Nazi terror and the front line of the Cold War, Berlin etched itself into history like no other city. Up until 1989, the Wall cruelly split Berlin right down the middle; almost two decades later, the scars have healed after a wave of massive building projects. This has been re-development on a grand scale, from the grand new **Spreebogen** government quarter to the new embassies around **Brandenburg Gate** and the soaring 'mini-city' of **Potsdamer Platz**. At the turn of the century, Berlin could boast it was Europe's largest building site, but change has not been confined to the major projects. Berlin has wit-nessed smaller-scale metamorphoses in its working-class districts of **Kreuzberg** and **Prenzlauer Berg**, while there are long-term plans to transform **Alexanderplatz**, the city's eastern hub, into something more aesthetically pleasing. West of the centre, the ruined **Kaiser Wilhelm Memorial Church**, as potent a symbol of Berlin as the Brandenburg Gate itself, is a poignant epitaph to the city's destruction in World War II. Its jagged silhouette pierces the skyline at the end of the **Kurfürstendamm** (usually shortened to **Ku'damm**), where Berliners pour their Euro into the classy shops and boutiques lining the capital's top shopping street. In the eastern city, newly fashionable Friedrichstraße is another quality retail area. For Berlin, the future has never been brighter.

TOP ATTRACTIONS

*** Brandenburg Gate: instantly recognized symbol of the once divided city.
*** Unter den Linden: gracious avenue, fine buildings.
*** Museums Island: a treasure trove of history.
*** Gendarmenmarkt: elegant square, twin cathedrals.
*** Schloß Charlottenburg: former royal palace.
*** Nikolaiviertel: recon-structed medieval quarter.
** Kaiser Wilhelm Memorial Church: reminder of wartime devastation.
** Kurfürstendamm: shopping and entertainment hub.

Opposite: *Steel sculpture frames the Kaiser Wilhelm Memorial Church.*

Above: *Cruise boats take visitors from the heart of Berlin to the scenic Wannsee lakes.*

FACT FILE

Geography: Berlin lies on the River Spree in the North European Plain. There are 200km (124 miles) of waterways within the city limits; the highest point is Grosse Müggelberg, at 115m (377ft).
Population: 3.4 million.
Area: Greater Berlin covers an area of 890km² (344 sq miles). It is 46km (29 miles) across and 38km (24 miles) north-south.
Language: German.
Administration: Berlin is divided into 12 boroughs, known as *Bezirke*, each with its own mayor.
Largest lake: Müggelsee. Others are Wannsee and Tegeler See.
Largest park: Tiergarten.

THE LAND

Berlin, spread out in the midst of the flat North European Plain, is Germany's largest and greenest city, with more than a third of its 890km² (344 sq miles) taken up by forests, woodlands, parks, lakes, rivers and canals. There is so much **water** in the ground, in fact – Berlin is built on a postglacial river bed – that it has to be drained before the foundations of the new high-rise buildings can be laid, hence the multicoloured pipes issuing from every building site in the city. There are almost 200km (124 miles) of navigable rivers and canals in Berlin, further indications of the city's water-borne environment.

In the west, the **River Havel** flows into the **Wannsee** lakes from **Tegeler See** in the north; at Spandau in the northwest, the Havel is joined by the **River Spree**, which meanders across the city from **Grosser Müggelsee** and the lakes of the southeast. Among the southeastern suburbs are the vast Treptower Park beside the Spree and, further out, the woods and waterways of Köpenick. Southwest of the centre, near the **forest** of Grunewald, are Berlin's very own sandy **beaches** along Wannsee. The green areas extend right into the heart of Berlin, where the wooded **Tiergarten**, between the Spree and the Landwehrkanal, makes a healthy contribution to the clarity of Berlin's air.

The **distance** across Greater Berlin from west to east is around 46km (29 miles) and from north to south about 38km (24 miles). The highest hill in Greater Berlin is **Grosse Müggelberg**, in the district of Köpenick, at just 115m (377ft); most smaller hills are man-made in the form of enormous mounds of rubble that were dumped during the rebuilding of Berlin after World War II.

BERLIN	J	F	M	A	M	J	J	A	S	O	N	D
AVERAGE TEMP. °F	30	32	39	48	57	63	66	65	59	49	41	34
AVERAGE TEMP. °C	-1	0	4	9	14	17	19	18	15	9	5	1
HOURS OF SUN DAILY	4	7	6	9	10	9	9	10	9	7	5	3
RAINFALL ins	1.8	1.6	1.3	1.7	1.9	2.6	2.9	2.7	1.9	1.9	1.8	1.7
RAINFALL mm	46	40	33	42	49	65	73	69	48	49	46	43
DAYS OF RAINFALL	17	15	12	13	12	13	14	14	12	14	16	15

Climate

Berlin's situation on the North European Plain endows it with a **continental climate** of extreme temperatures – it can be bitterly cold in winter and surprisingly warm in high summer. The in-between seasons of spring, when the city's 400,000 trees are bursting into bud, and autumn, when the leaves are turning gold, are particularly good times to visit.

Summer in Berlin can be a delight, with numerous parks and gardens to enjoy, and lakes and rivers for boating. In the warmest months of July and August, the temperature regularly tops 20°C (68°F) and often hits 25°C (77°F).

In the **coldest months** of the year, January and February, the east wind sweeping in from Russia sometimes sends the temperature plummeting to minus 10°C (14°F) or below – but it is not always like that. Many days see temperatures around 5°C (41°F). When the **snow** comes, as it usually does, it doesn't stay for long.

Below: *The splendid wooded Tiergarten in the centre of Berlin was once a royal hunting ground.*

WHAT THEY SAID

Purveyors of the written word have had their say about Berlin over the years:

• The poet **Johann Wolfgang Goethe** (1749–1832): 'There live there bold people, such that one does not get far by being delicate. One must be sharp-tongued and sometimes a little coarse to keep one's head above water.'

• The writer **Georg Forster** (1754–94): 'Berlin is certainly one of the most beautiful cities in Europe.'

• The poet **Friedrich Schiller** (1759–1805): 'That a longer stay in Berlin would enable me to make progress in my artistic work I do not doubt for a moment.'

• Journalist **Kurt Tucholsky** (1890–1935): 'Youth here is never at a loss for words – then Berlin seems forever young, and ever younger.'

The Boroughs

The first documented mention of Berlin was in 1244, following its merger with neighbouring Cölln. Today the **State of Berlin**, which sits within the **Federal State of Brandenburg**, comprises 12 boroughs – until 2001 there were 23 municipal districts. The boroughs are (broadly west to east) Spandau, Reinickendorf, Charlottenburg-Wilmersdorf, Steglitz-Zehlendorf, Mitte, Tempelhof-Schöneberg, Friedrichshain-Kreuzberg, Pankow, Neukölln, Lichtenberg, Marzahn-Hellersdorf and Treptow-Köpenick.

Visitors to Berlin will spend most of their time in the **central districts** of Charlottenburg, Tiergarten, Mitte, Prenzlauer Berg and Kreuzberg. Given enough time, they may also take in the districts of Schöneberg, Wilmersdorf and Friedrichshain. **Further out** and awaiting discovery on a longer visit are (clockwise from the west) Spandau, Reinickendorf, Wedding, Pankow, Weissensee, Hohenschönhausen, Marzahn, Lichtenberg, Hellersdorf, Köpenick, Treptow, Neukölln, Tempelhof, Steglitz and Zehlendorf.

Following nearly 40 years of partition that ended in 1989, the city of Berlin still has two distinct identities – a situation that will probably exist for a long time to come. The districts of Charlottenburg and Tiergarten formed the heart of the former **West Berlin** and remain the capital's prime shopping location. The core of the old **East Berlin**

was Mitte, and today this remains Berlin's cultural focus, with many of the city's leading museums, art galleries and musical venues located here.

Some streets and squares in the eastern part of the city have been renamed to reflect its altered political status. An example is the **renaming** of Marx-Engels-Platz in the central Mitte district as Schloßplatz.

HISTORY IN BRIEF

Though Slavic races occupied the site of present-day Berlin from the 6th century, the city has existed for rather less time. Its history can be traced back to the early 12th century, with the founding of **Berlin** and **Cölln** as small **trading posts** at a crossing point on the River Spree.

The earliest recorded documentary reference to Cölln was in 1237 and to Berlin seven years later; Berlin was granted city status in 1251 and Cölln in 1261, the communities merging in 1307 to become Berlin-Cölln (the name was shortened to Berlin in 1709 with the incorporation of Friedrichswerder and Dorotheenstadt), with a population of some 8000.

The **merger**, aimed at strengthening Brandenburg's stand against the robber barons, was legalized in the courthouse that stood in today's Nikolaiviertel quarter – the spot is identified in front of the **Nikolaikirche** (St Nicholas Church). By then, Berlin had adopted the **bear** as its symbol, probably because of the similarity of the words – the German for bear is *Bär*.

Berlin prospered during the early 14th century and in 1359 joined the **Hanseatic League**, a group of trading cities. Though it clung to its autonomy within the German empire, the city came under the influence of the **Hohenzollern** family, who controlled the March of Brandenburg under **Elector Friedrich I**, and forfeited its independence.

Above: *The heraldic Berlin bear appears on the city's crest, and there are bears in Berlin's zoo.*
Opposite: *Aerial view of Berlin – the German capital is 46km (29 miles) across.*

THE BERLIN BEAR

Berlin's heraldic bear first appeared on the city's seal in 1280 – there were in fact two bears, probably representing **Berlin** and its twin town of **Cölln** across the River Spree. Menaced by the eagle of **Elector Friedrich II** on his 15th-century seal, the bear appeared on successive coats of arms before finally being permitted to wear a mural **crown** as the symbol of a free town in the mid-1800s. Not until after Berlin's installation as the capital of the German Empire in the 1870s did the bear lose its degrading collar.

Above: *Gladiators atop the gateway to Schloß Charlottenburg, Berlin's splendid Baroque palace.*

THE SOLDIER KING

Such were the militaristic ambitions of **Friedrich Wilhelm I**, who ruled from 1713–40, that he spent his life in uniform and to his subjects became known as the *Soldatenkönig* (Soldier King). A frugal man, he had no time for the arts or anything artistic, and early in his reign banished ballet and other musical performances. He turned the **Lustgarten** (Pleasure Garden) in front of the Royal Palace into a parade ground and even replaced the decorative flowers in the grounds of **Schloß Charlottenburg** with a more useful crop – cabbages.

The Hohenzollerns

The reign of Elector Friedrich II, from 1440–70, saw Berliners become subjects of the Hohenzollerns. A brand-new **coat of arms**, which showed the Berlin bear being menaced by the claws of the Hohenzollern eagle, clearly showed Berlin's citizens what was expected of them. **Friedrich II** dissolved the city council and demolished the town hall. Subsequently, when the people rebelled in the **Berliner Unwillen** (Berlin Indignation) uprising of 1448, they were completely crushed by the Hohenzollern militia. It was the Berliners' last attempt at salvaging full independence.

But their independent spirit survived and in 1539, at the time of the **Reformation**, they persuaded the ruling **Elector Joachim II** to convert to **Lutheranism** as a way of not having to pay the Catholic Church tax. By the mid-16th century, Berlin's population had risen to 12,000, but expansion was halted by the **Thirty Years' War** (1618–48), which left it with a population of only 6000 and a third of the city in ruins.

The bloody war started out as a **religious conflict** between the Catholics and the Protestants and then developed into a full-scale confrontation involving the troops of three countries – Germany, Austria and Sweden. The **Peace of Westphalia** eventually restored order, but by then approximately half of Berlin's population had fled from the city.

The Huguenots

In an effort to rebuild Berlin's decimated population, **Elector Friedrich Wilhelm** – the 'Great Elector', who ruled from 1640–88 – encouraged well-off Jewish families from **Vienna** to settle in Berlin in 1671, and also allowed in some 6000 Huguenots fleeing **France** in 1685 after **Louis XIV** had revoked the **Edict of Nantes** that guaranteed them religious freedom. From 6000 people in 1650, Berlin's population soared to 36,000 within 50 years and to 172,000 by 1800.

During this time, Berlin further developed its role as a trading city, producing textiles and weapons, and the completion of the **Oder-Spree Canal** in 1668 gave it added significance.

Berlin was also developing as an **academic centre**. Encouraged by his wife **Sophie Charlotte** to found the Academy of Arts and the Academy of Sciences, the Great Elector's heir, **Elector Friedrich III**, proclaimed himself 'King Friedrich I of Prussia' in 1701. Some elegant buildings remain from his reign – they include the Queen's palace, **Schloß Charlottenburg**.

Culture and **King Friedrich Wilhelm I**, who ruled from 1713–40, never really went together. His passion lay in building a mighty army – an ambition that caused thousands to flee to avoid being called up. It took the ascension to the throne of **Friedrich II** in 1740 to recapture the good times – he restored Berlin's cultural image and was responsible for Unter den Linden and also many fine buildings. His 1748 conquest of Silesia, now part of Poland, earned him the tag **Frederick the Great**.

FREDERICK THE GREAT

Berlin was never favoured by the flute-playing Friedrich II (1712–86), King of Prussia from 1740 until his death. Known to his subjects as **'Old Fritz'**, he much preferred his out-of-town palaces at Potsdam: **Schloß Sanssouci** and **Neues Palais**; he corresponded with French philosopher and writer **François Voltaire**, who stayed at Sanssouci from 1750–53 at the king's invitation. A competent administrator and first-class general, he raised Prussia's international profile; his seizure of **Silesia** from Austria in the 1740s served to strengthen Prussian military might.

Below: *Frederick the Great is buried at Schloß Sanssouci.*

WILHELM VON HUMBOLDT

The elegant neoclassical **Humboldt University** on Unter den Linden takes its name from the philologist-statesman Wilhelm von Humboldt. In 1810, with the support of his younger brother **Alexander**, he founded a secondary school in the building, which had been completed 60 years earlier as a royal palace for **Friedrich II**; it was transformed into Berlin's first university soon afterwards and renamed after its founder in 1946. Seated **statues** of the brothers guard the university, which through the years has had many **Nobel Prize** winners among its staff.

Napoleon's Conquest

On Frederick the Great's death in 1786, Berlin went into decline through the weak policies and high spending of his nephew **Friedrich Wilhelm II**, who held power from 1786–97. It was left to his son, **Friedrich Wilhelm III** (1797–1840) to deal with Napoleon's advance across Europe that swept him through Prussia in October 1806. On his way into an undefended Berlin, Napoleon took a liking to the **Quadriga statue** above the **Brandenburg Gate** and during the two-year French occupation had it carted off to Paris (it was, however, returned in 1814). The Prussian army got its own back on Napoleon in 1813, joining forces with the Russians and Austrians to triumph at the **Battle of Leipzig**.

Meanwhile, Berlin's **cultural** aspirations had been given a boost by the opening in 1810 of the new **university** founded by Wilhelm von Humboldt. From then on Berlin really started to make a name for itself in the fields of art, literature and architecture.

Industrial progress was spawning a new working class and in March 1848 Berliners – as elsewhere in Germany – revolted against the Prussian authorities, demanding improved living and working conditions and freedom of press and speech. The **protests** were met with military force, leaving more than 200 dead. Though minor concessions were granted at first, they were followed by a renewed clampdown.

Right: *The neoclassical Humboldt University building was designed as a royal palace.*

Left: *A statue of the 'Iron Chancellor', Otto von Bismarck, graces the Tiergarten.*

The Empire's Capital

From around the mid-19th century, Berlin was transformed into Europe's chief **industrial city**, attracting thousands of workers who, by 1871, had helped to swell the population to 827,000. In 1862, **Otto von Bismarck** was appointed chancellor by **King Wilhelm I**; he quickly set about achieving unity among the German states and, led by the Prussians, they achieved notable victories over Austria in 1866 and in the **Franco-Prussian War** five years later in which Bismarck took Alsace-Lorraine. **Unification of the German states** became inevitable and in June 1871 the German Empire came into being with Berlin as its capital.

Berlin's elevated status gave it instant appeal to industrialists and the population quickly passed the million mark. In 1871 alone, an extra 134,000 people crowded into Berlin; most incomers were housed in the wretched tenement blocks that were dubbed *Mietskasernen* (rent barracks). In 1888, Wilhelm I's sick son **Friedrich III** ruled for just 99 days, to be followed by the third and last Kaiser, **Wilhelm II**, who piloted the German Reich into World War I.

In the meantime, Berlin's infrastructural growth continued apace: the first electric **tram** ran in 1881 and the first **U-Bahn** underground train in 1902. **Cars** appeared in the streets in 1905 and in 1913 the **Avus**, Germany's first **Autobahn**, was opened in the southwest of the city.

THE IRON CHANCELLOR

Otto Eduard Leopold von Bismarck (1815–98) was the German Empire's architect in chief. He gained significant experience in European affairs as Prussian ambassador in **St Petersburg** (1859–62) and subsequently **Paris** before returning to **Berlin** as chief Prussian minister and engineering the defeat of Austria in 1866 and France in the Franco-Prussian War of 1870–71. With Prussia at the head of a united Germany, Bismarck became the 'Iron Chancellor' of **Kaiser Wilhelm I**, presiding over the Berlin Congress of European powers in 1878. He did not enjoy life in Berlin and tried unsuccessfully to move the government to Potsdam. He was dismissed as chancellor by **Kaiser Wilhelm II** in 1890.

World War I

The Great War that engulfed Europe proved the last military campaign of the Hohenzollerns. The Kaiser was enthusiastically cheered outside the **Berliner Schloß** as Germany mobilized for war in August 1914, but the huge loss of life and their heavily rationed existence turned Berliners against the campaign. A series of strikes preceded Germany's capitulation and with humiliating defeat came instability. Following Kaiser Wilhelm II's abdication on 9 November 1918, ending 500 years of Hohenzollern rule, confusion reigned: in the Reichstag, Social Democrat **Philipp Scheidemann** proclaimed the formation of the **German Republic**, while from the balcony of the Berliner Schloß, Spartacus League leader **Karl Liebknecht** proclaimed a **socialist republic**. In the period of bitter SPD-communist rivalry that followed, Liebknecht and fellow communist Rosa Luxemburg were murdered in the **Spartacus Revolt** of 15 January 1919 by the reactionary **Freikorps** militia – effectively the forerunners of Hitler's stormtroopers.

While turmoil raged in Berlin, the new proponents of democracy decamped 220km (137 miles) southwest to Weimar, where they drew up a constitution for the new **Weimar Republic** – it was adopted in July 1919. But the new order lacked stability and eight months later Berlin witnessed the short-lived and unsuccessful Kapp putsch, a revolt led by right-wing civil servant **Wolfgang Kapp**.

Amid outbursts of political violence on the streets, Berlin's population doubled to almost four million in 1920, with the incorporation of eight towns and a number of smaller communities into a Greater Berlin. Throughout the decade the German capital developed a reputation for the **arts** and **theatre** in particular; it was a vibrant and exciting city to visit and nowhere in Europe had more appeal.

DEATH IN BERLIN

The German communist party was only a fortnight old when its two leaders, **Karl Liebknecht** and **Rosa Luxemburg**, were kidnapped from their hiding place at Mannheimer Straße in Berlin's Wilmersdorf district on the evening of 15 January 1919. Right-wing **Freikorps** members took them to a hotel near the Zoo being used by a pro-government army division, where they were interrogated and beaten before being led away one at a time. Liebknecht was shot, allegedly trying to escape, while Luxemburg was given the same treatment and her body thrown into the **Landwehrkanal** – the spot is marked by a plaque.

Turbulent Thirties

The high spending of the 'golden Twenties' was accompanied by absurdly **high inflation**. In mid-1923 a US dollar bought 150,000 Reichsmark; by the end of the year it bought 12 billion Reichsmark. **Chancellor Gustav Stresemann** introduced the Rentenmark (each one replaced a billion Reichsmark) and slowly the economy recovered. But an unsavoury backdrop to Berlin's social hedonism was increasing **political friction** between left and right extremists, fuelled by increasing **unemployment** – by 1932, some 600,000 were out of work.

In May 1930, **street rioting** in Berlin between the communists and members of Adolf Hitler's fast-rising NSDAP, the **National Socialist German Workers' Party**, cost 30 lives. In the Reichstag elections of July 1932 the **Nazis** claimed almost 40 per cent of the seats. Hitler's eventual appointment as chancellor was marked by a torchlight parade through the Brandenburg Gate on 30 January 1933. The burning of the Reichstag on 27 February (see box, this page) provided a pretext to banish all opposition parties. From March 1933 the Nazis had absolute control and when president Paul Hindenburg died in 1934, Hitler added the title **Führer** to that of Chancellor.

Berlin was the power base of the **Third Reich** and concentration camps set up to incarcerate political opponents were soon being filled by members of Berlin's 150,000-strong **Jewish community**. Hitler's hatred of the Jews manifested itself in *Kristallnacht* (night of broken glass) on 9 November 1938 (see box, page 60); by the start of World War II, Berlin's Jewish population had been halved.

REICHSTAG FIRE

The night of 27 February 1933 climaxed Germany's last 'free' election campaign until after World War II. Setting fire to the Reichstag building was widely held to be the work of the **Nazis**, but a young Dutch communist, **Marius van der Lubbe**, was arrested at the scene and shouldered the blame; he was executed a year later. The seat of the fire was the debating chamber beneath the glass roof dome – the blaze could be seen all over Berlin. The fire provided **Hitler** with the excuse he needed to round up political opponents and many were sent to their deaths.

Opposite: *The Marx-Engels sculpture recalls 40 years of communism.* **Below:** *Sir Norman Foster's glass dome surmounts the Reichstag.*

SHATTERED CITY

A quarter of Berlin's buildings were destroyed by **Allied bombs** in World War II. Of the city's 1.5 million homes, 600,000 were wrecked and a further 100,000 severely damaged. By the end of the war, Berlin's **population** had been reduced to 2.3 million, just over half the prewar figure; around 750,000 of its citizens had fled, many of them during the last stages of the conflict.

World War II

When Germany attacked **Poland** on 1 September 1939, Berliners received the news with little enthusiasm. The excesses of the 1920s had given way to a decade of political extremes, and Nazi power lust had been leading inexorably to war. On 25 August 1940, 22 tons of bombs fell on Berlin – the **Allies**' first direct action against the city and retaliation to the **Luftwaffe's bombing of London**. More than 200 Berliners had died in air raids by the end of 1940; throughout the war, bombing claimed the lives of at least 50,000.

From November 1943, bombing continued night after night – even the zoo was hit, but remained open. Hitler's boast in his early years contained a bitter truth: 'Just give me 10 years and you won't recognize your cities.' By mid-March 1944, the **assault on Berlin** had left 6000 dead, 20,000 seriously injured and 1.5 million homeless. An area of 9km^2 (3.5 sq miles) had been flattened. In October, raids by British and American aircraft resumed in earnest and by mid-1945 one in three homes in Berlin had been left uninhabitable.

Meanwhile, the **Russians** were planning their assault from the east and on 21 April 1945 the Red Army entered what was left of the ruined German capital. The destroyed city fell on 2 May, and just six days later came Germany's official **surrender**.

Left: *Architect Daniel Libeskind was responsible for the striking design of the Jewish Museum.*
Opposite: *The bomb-shattered spire of the Kaiser Wilhelm Memorial Church stands as a monument to the horrors of war.*

The Berlin Airlift

At the 1945 **Potsdam Conference**, the four-power agreement split responsibility for Berlin among the Allies. The **British**, **French** and **Americans** took control of the city's western part, while the **Soviets** occupied the east – almost half the city's total area. The 1946 elections gave Berliners their first free ballot since Hitler came to power; the **Social Democrats**' victory set alarm bells ringing in the east of the city. Perceiving the Western occupation forces as a threat to Soviet security and capitalist West Berlin as exerting a bad influence, the Soviets engineered a **blockade**. They perceived that only by starving Berlin into submission would the entire city ever be totally in Soviet hands.

On 24 June 1948, the Soviets cut all links with West Germany, effectively sealing off West Berlin from the rest of the world. The following day the Berlin Airlift started – an amazing operation that was to last 11 months as a number of British and American aircraft flew in round the clock, bringing up to 8000 tons of food, fuel, machinery and other necessary supplies daily from air bases in **Hamburg**, **Hanover** and **Frankfurt**. When the Soviets at last lifted the blockade in May 1949, it had been at a cost of 78 lives.

While West Berlin retained its ties with the newly founded **Federal Republic of Germany** (FRG), East Berlin was declared the capital of the new communist **German Democratic Republic** (GDR) – the former Soviet zone.

HITLER'S LAST DAYS

From mid-January 1945, Hitler confined himself to the **Berlin Chancellory** and the huge underground **bunker** within its grounds – it held a staff of 600. He made his last **radio broadcast** on 30 January. Soon the **Red Army** was within striking distance of the city and by 23 April they were in the suburbs. With time running out, Hitler married his long-time friend **Eva Braun** in the bunker on Sunday 29 April, following her arrival from Munich, where she had been for much of the war. The following afternoon, with the Chancellory under attack, they chewed on their cyanide capsules in a joint act of suicide. The two bodies were then set alight and buried in the Chancellory garden.

Above: *Memorial crosses pay tribute to those who lost their lives in unsuccessful attempts to flee to the West.*

VICTIMS OF THE WALL

Around 190 people died seeking their freedom in the 28 years that the **Wall** divided Berlin. Many reached freedom by sprinting, scrambling or swimming over the border, often under fire. Some tunnelled and some escaped by light aircraft; two winched their way above the wall on a cable stretched between rooftops. The last victim of the Wall was engineer **Winfried Freudenberg**, whose body was found suspended from an oak tree in the district of **Zehlendorf**; on 8 March 1989, he escaped from East Berlin by balloon but, in danger of crossing back into East Germany, had to make a forced landing – a manoeuvre that cost him his life.

Towards the Wall

Berliners who found themselves in the Soviet sector after the city's partition soon discovered their fellow citizens in the west were better off. With the GDR only four years old, 1000 people a day were crossing to the west and the fledgling state was losing many higher qualified workers. Matters came to a bloody head on 17 June 1953, when building workers on the new **Stalinallee** boulevard (now Karl Marx Allee) led a nationwide revolt against the government of **Walter Ulbricht**; the rebellion was crushed by Soviet tanks, leaving many dead and 4000 arrested. The avenue west of the Brandenburg Gate was renamed **Straße des 17 Juni** in commemoration.

The exodus of skilled workers, at a huge cost to the new GDR state, continued throughout the 1950s. By 1960, with east-west friction increasing, 2.5 million East Germans had fled to the west. Under orders from Soviet leader **Nikita Khrushchev** to close the border, the East German authorities set to work on the night of 12–13 August 1961 with rolls of barbed wire and road blocks. The reinforced concrete **Wall** soon replaced the temporary barricades and some 190 would-be refugees were to lose their lives in escape attempts. Border crossings were established for foreigners, including **Checkpoint Charlie** in the American sector.

A Unified Berlin

The date 9 November 1989 remains etched on the minds of Berlin's 3.4 million inhabitants – the day the **border reopened** after 28 long years of division. It was the high point of a year in which thousands of East Germans had fled to the west through Hungary, Poland and Czechoslovakia; a year in which Soviet leader **Mikhail**

Gorbachev, in Berlin for East Germany's 40th anniversary celebrations, told GDR chief **Erich Honecker** that he could no longer rely on Soviet tanks to maintain order. The writing, so to speak, was on the wall.

Ten days later, on 17 October, Honecker resigned to be replaced by deputy **Egon Krenz**. He promised reforms, but on 4 November a crowd of 800,000 herded into **Alexanderplatz** to vent their wrath on the GDR leadership. Their point was well made: on the evening of 9 November the GDR broadcast an end to foreign travel restrictions and euphoric East Berliners hit the streets in their thousands, aiming to be among the first to go through the Wall to a rapturous welcome in the west. Within 24 hours, 100,000 East Berliners had sampled life in the west.

On 3 October 1990, the Allies forfeited their role as occupying powers and Germany at last became a **sovereign nation** again with the absorption of the former GDR. Following reunification, Berlin was restored as Germany's **capital** and in May 1999 the city resumed as the seat of government.

HISTORICAL CALENDAR

1237: Cölln, a twin settlement opposite Berlin on the River Spree, is mentioned for the first time in documentary records.
1244: Berlin is mentioned for the first time in records.
1618–48: Thirty Years' War destroys Berlin and the population of Berlin/Cölln is reduced to 6000.
1740–86: Under Frederick the Great, Berlin becomes one of the great European cities.
1806: Napoleon occupies Berlin.
1871: Berlin becomes capital of the German Empire. With a booming economy, the population reaches one million.
1914–18: The Great War, after which Kaiser Wilhelm II abdicates, paving the way for a German Republic.
1920–30: The 'Golden Twenties' highlights art, culture and entertainment in the Greater Berlin, now with four million inhabitants.
1936: Berlin hosts the Nazi showpiece Olympic Games.
1939–45: World War II leaves Berlin in ruins with 50,000 Berliners dead. The city is divided into occupation zones administered by the four Allies.
1948: The Soviet blockade of Berlin. An Allied airlift lasting 11 months keeps the city alive.
1949: Berlin becomes the capital of the new German Democratic Republic.
1961: The Wall is built, dividing the city into East and West Berlin.
1989: Collapse of the Berlin Wall.
1991: Berlin is proclaimed the capital of a reunited Germany.
1994: The last occupying forces formally leave Berlin.
1999: German government departments relocate from Bonn; Berlin is once again Germany's political capital.

Below: *The black, red and gold bands of the German flag again stand for the whole country.*

TOURIST CITY

Berlin is Germany's most important **tourism destination**, receiving some 7.1 million visitors annually. They stay for an average of 2.3 days, recording almost 16 million overnight stays each year. The city has some 85,000 **beds** available to visitors; up to 100,000 **jobs** are directly related to the tourism industry. With an annual turnover of €4.35 billion (£3 billion), tourism ranks as the fifth largest sector of Berlin's economy.

Below: *Souvenirs of the former East German state attract visitors near the Brandenburg Gate.*

GOVERNMENT AND ECONOMY

When the Wall came down in 1989, Europe's political leaders were quick to express concern at what effect the rapid turn of events would have on European stability and security. Full **German reunification** was then seen as inevitable but some way off, and the prospect of a much-enlarged Germany, shifting the balance within the European Community, alarmed politicians in all member states. In the event, the two Germanys became one in less than a year with a combined population of almost 80 million, and the ensuing problems were internal rather than external.

In his capacity as chancellor of the Community's largest member, **Helmut Kohl** was charged with merging two divergent economies. While **East Germany** had been a leading industrial producer of the old Soviet bloc, 40 per cent of its foreign trade had been with the USSR and its economy was way behind that of the successful **Federal Republic**. Full economic integration was to prove a lasting headache. In addition, East German industry desperately needed substantial investment to bring it up to western standards, and in the 1990s something like US$1000 billion was ploughed into rebuilding the former GDR.

The New Priority

Unemployment, unknown in the GDR, spread in the east of the country as the former East Germany converted to a market-driven economy, with an attendant lack of job security. There was some pressure on jobs in Berlin as East Berliners chose to resettle in western parts of the city – they were initially entitled to **subsidies** that placed a considerable financial burden on the Bonn government. When **Gerhard Schröder** succeeded Helmut Kohl as German chancellor in 1998, at the head of the Social Democrat/Greens coalition government, 4.4 million (11 per cent of the workforce) were **unemployed** – the highest level since the bad times of the Weimar Republic. With benefit costs pushing Germany's **national debt** to its highest postwar levels, reducing that figure became an urgent priority of the new administration.

Above: *River Spree cruise boat passes the new Hauptbahnhof (main railway station).*

Meanwhile, as a founding member of the Community – now the European Union – Germany has steadfastly played the role of 'good European'. On 1 January 1999, it was one of 11 EU nations to welcome the **Euro** enthusiastically, viewing currency harmonization as an essential step on the road to full **political union** within Europe.

Jobs for the Masses

The relocation of federal government departments from Bonn to Berlin this century has created a wave of new jobs, and between them the federal and state administrations now employ around 250,000 people. New office developments like those at **Potsdamer Platz**, **Leipziger Platz** and **Friedrichstraße** have also created work, while the **tourism** sector – more than seven million people visit Berlin each year – is employing ever-increasing numbers in hotels and related enterprises.

KEEP TRAVELLING

Of special interest to keen travellers, Berlin's biggest fair, the *Internationale Tourismus Börse* (ITB-Berlin), is continental Europe's largest **travel show**, filling all 30-odd halls of the **Berlin Exhibition Grounds** for a week in early March. There is nothing on this scale elsewhere in Europe to which members of the public are invited. Exhibitors come from pretty well every country in the world – at least, those that welcome tourists – so it is a good venue at which to plan your next holiday.

THE PEOPLE

No German city is as cosmopolitan as Berlin. Since the arrival of Jewish immigrants from **Vienna** and **French Huguenots** in the late 17th century, Berlin has opened its doors to successive waves of incomers – **Bohemians** in the 18th century, **Jews** in the 19th century, and **Russians**, **Greeks**, **Italians** and **Turks** in the 20th century. The Turks live mostly in the Kreuzberg district, where they comprise nearly a fifth of the population, and also in Wedding and Neukölln; since their arrival in the 1960s, their numbers have grown to 150,000 and they constitute by far the largest immigrant community – a third of Berlin's foreign workers are Turkish. In the past two decades, Berlin has taken in many former **Eastern Bloc** citizens – from **Romania** in particular. In the former East Berlin, the 10,000 or so **Vietnamese** constituted the largest group of immigrant workers. Under Allied occupation from the end of the war until the early 1990s, West Berlin was home to **Anglo-American** forces.

Berlin people have always regarded themselves as Berliners first and Germans second – a characteristic strengthened during the years of geographical **isolation** behind the Wall, when a fortress mentality was all-pervasive. It was the Berliners' spirit and self-belief that saw them through years of adversity – the cruelty of the Nazi era, the catastrophe of World War II, the Russian blockade and the divisions of the Cold War.

SAFE CITY?

Berlin is essentially a safe city in which to travel about, though the usual **common-sense rules** apply. Walking at night should not pose a problem, though it is wise to steer clear of eastern Berlin's grimmer housing estates. The rise of the **neo-Nazi** movement and their aggression towards foreigners should not be ignored; do not do or say anything to incite trouble. Mugging on Berlin's streets is rare, but it helps not to give the appearance of being enormously wealthy.

Religion

While Berlin's present cultural mix makes it something of a religious melting pot, the city has remained **Protestant** first and foremost since the Reformation. Its Protestant population inceased rapidly in the 1800s and now Protestants outnumber **Catholics** in the city by three to one. **Muslims** make up Berlin's next largest religious community; there are 200,000 followers of Islam in the city, nearly 10 per cent of the German total, and most of them Turkish immigrants. The city's **Jewish** population was decimated in World War II and now numbers just 12,000 from a prewar total of 150,000.

Language

As in any country the world over, a little effort to speak the native language goes a long way. **German** is distantly related to **English** and is the first language of more than 100 million people. Teaching of English is now compulsory in German schools, and in Berlin you will generally find yourself understood – but maybe less so in the eastern part of the city, where **Russian** was taught in preference to English in GDR days.

SAY IT IN GERMAN

German **pronunciation** is not difficult, once you have grasped a few basics. Silent letters are extemely rare and **consonants** sound as in English with a handful of exceptions – most importantly, the German 'j' sounds like the English 'y'; 'st' is pronounced 'sht'; 'sp' is pronounced 'shp'; 'v' sounds like an English 'f', and 'w' like an English 'v'. The German 'z' is pronounced 'ts'. The hard 's' (pronounced as in the English 'miss') is written either 'ss' or 'ß'. The main **vowel** differences concern use of the umlaut (¨): ä as in lair, äu as in toy, ö as in burn and ü as in tune. (See box on page 123 for some useful phrases.)

Opposite: *A puppet seller attracts a youngster's attention in the western city centre.*
Left: *These preserved ceiling mosaics are on view at the Kaiser Wilhelm Memorial Church.*

SCHINKEL INFLUENCE

Karl Friedrich Schinkel was Berlin's foremost neoclassical **architect**. Born in 1781, he launched his artistic career in painting in the early 1800s before combining his talents for architecture and stage design. His finest works include the **Neue Wache** (New Guardhouse) and **Altes Museum** (Old Museum) on Unter den Linden, the **Berlin Concert Hall** on Gendarmenmarkt, the **Schinkel Pavilion** at **Schloß Charlottenburg**, and the neo-Gothic **Napoleonic war memorial** in **Viktoria Park**, Kreuzberg. He died in 1841.

Architecture

Given the scale of Berlin's wartime devastation, it is perhaps surprising there are so many attractive buildings to admire in the city today – and in such a **range of styles**, from Medieval through Gothic, Baroque, Renaissance and neoclassical to *Jugendstil* (Art Nouveau). A massive repair and **reconstruction** programme in the postwar years has given Berlin back much of its lost glory. While a lot of what you see may not be original, it is as close a likeness as you will get. The good news is that the majority of Berlin's most attractive buildings have been given breathing space; they are not hemmed in by high-rise offices as they are in many other cities.

Many of Berlin's finest buildings date from the late 17th century to the early 19th century and were the inspired work of the city's three great architects – **Georg von Knobelsdorff** (1699–1753), **Carl Gotthard Langhans**

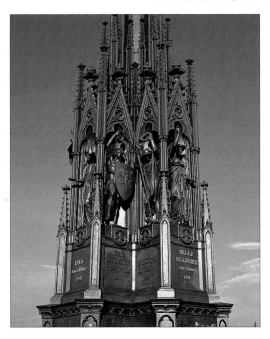

(1732–1808) and **Karl Friedrich Schinkel** (1781–1841). Knobelsdorff (*see* box, page 37) was the court architect of Frederick the Great; his greatest creations, inspired by visits abroad, include the Sanssouci Palace, the National Opera House on Unter den Linden, and St Hedwig's Cathedral. Langhans is best known for styling Berlin's erstwhile symbol, the Brandenburg Gate, while Schinkel (*see* box, this page) had few peers among neoclassical designers.

Each era of Berlin history left its architectural mark. The 1930s bequeathed the Nazi-built **Air Ministry** of Hermann Göring and the **Olympic Stadium**, while in the 1950s came **Stalin-allee's** Soviet-inspired showpiece apartments. Many of eastern Berlin's featureless **housing estates** were a legacy of the 1970s, while creations of the 1990s and 2000s include the impressive glass-and-steel offices of revived **Potsdamer Platz**.

Theatre

Berlin's theatre scene comes in two halves – it is split between the west and east of the city centre. Venues in the western part are centred around the **Ku'damm**; in the eastern part they are spread out north and west of **Friedrichstraße station**. The most interesting venues are in the east – for instance the **Berliner Ensemble**, concentrating on Bertolt Brecht and Shakespeare classics, and the **Deutsches Theater**, known for the quality of its productions both classic and modern. Another eastern venue of note is the **Maxim Gorki Theater**, which focuses mainly on Russian works, but also produces works by a variety of European playwrights.

Variety and musical performances first appeared on Berlin's theatre scene more than 100 years ago, and today venues such as the **Wintergarten** are keeping alive the arts of juggling, magic and acrobatics. The **Friedrichstadtpalast**, meanwhile, is Europe's largest revue theatre with a reputation to match. There is a touch of Broadway glamour at the **Theater des Westens**, which steers clear of international hit shows of the type staged by the **Schiller-Theater** and instead stages classics and home-produced musicals – imagination and creative flair are the bywords here.

Berlin boasts more than 500 **independent theatre groups** and around 20 performances are in production at any one time; seek out local listings.

Above: *Marlene Dietrich made her debut at the Deutsches Theater.*
Opposite: *Monument to the Wars of Liberation in Kreuzberg's Viktoria Park.*

MARLENE DIETRICH

Born on 27 December 1901, **Marie Magdalena von Losch** lived her early years in **Schöneberg**. She made her stage debut at the **Deutsches Theater** in 1922; after many appearances in silent films, her seductive role eight years later in *Der Blaue Engel* (The Blue Angel) elevated her to stardom. With the Nazis in power, she remained in **America**, scaling down film appearances after the war in favour of live cabaret. She died at the age of 90, and her name is freshly immortalized in Marlene-Dietrich-Platz at the heart of the new **Potsdamer Platz** development.

Music

Few cities can match Berlin for the variety of musical performance, and hardly any offer as many excellent venues. Whatever your musical preference, Berlin satisfies – from an orchestral concert in the acoustically correct **Berliner Philharmonie** to upbeat techno power at the ever-popular **SO36** venue in downtown Kreuzberg.

For **classical music** and **opera**, keep an eye on what is happening at the Philharmonie, the Deutsche Staatsoper (National Opera House) and Komische Oper on Unter den Linden, and the Konzerthaus Berlin (Berlin Concert Hall) on Gendarmenmarkt. Works of the great **German composers** feature regularly: Händel, Bach, Beethoven, Schumann, Mendelssohn, Brahms, Wagner and more. Quality venues for **jazz** enthusiasts include A-Trane at Savignyplatz and Quasimodo in Kantstraße; **club** fans could do worse than check out Linientreu in Budapester Straße or Oxymoron among the courtyards of Hackesche Höfe.

Art and Sculpture

Fine art began to flourish in Berlin from the early 18th century, largely through the efforts of the ruling Hohenzollerns. Chief among the romantic painters was **Caspar David Friedrich**, an exponent of wild landscape art, while **Max Liebermann** led the field of late 19th-century Impressionism, later helping to found the Berlin Secession movement. In the early 1900s, the abstract Expressionism art form took root in Berlin; among its proponents was **Käthe Kollwitz**, the Berlin artist whose work embraced many aspects of visual art.

SPORTING BERLIN

Berlin's bid to host the 2000 **Olympic Games** was an effort to eclipse the 1936 Games staged three years after the Nazis had seized power. The bid failed, but the city has pressed ahead with the creation of new sporting venues. The Olympic Stadium was given a costly facelift and reopened in 2004, while the new **Max Schmeling Hall** in Prenzlauer Berg is pulling in big crowds for its **dance festival** and **basketball** events. The **Berlin Marathon** attracts a large entry in late summer. The modernized **Hoppegarten** racetrack stages **horse-race** meetings.

Sculpture achieved fresh prominence from the late 17th century through the work of **Andreas Schlüter**, whose 22 warriors' death masks adorn a courtyard of the Zeughaus; **Johann Gottfried Schadow**, who designed the famous Quadriga atop the Brandenburg Gate; and **Christian Daniel Rauch**, whose splendid statue of Frederick the Great looks down Unter den Linden.

Literature

The period of German Enlightenment opened the book on Berlin's literary heritage late in the 18th century, fuelled by the output of dramatist **Gotthold Ephraim Lessing** (1729–81). Enlightenment evolved into Romanticism and the works of **Heinrich von Kleist** (1777–1811); in the mid-19th century, Realism took over and the novels of **Theodor Fontane** (1819–98) (*see* box, this page) captured the life of Berlin's high society. Naturalism became the literary focus at the turn of the century, marked by Nobel Prizewinner **Gerhart Hauptmann's** (1862–1946) effective portrayals of Berlin's working class.

THEODOR FONTANE

Theodor Fontane (1819–98), whose novels made a huge impact on 19th-century literary Realism in Germany, started his working life as an apprentice **pharmacist**, turning to **journalism** in 1849 to provide the basis for his **fiction writing**. His first major novel, *Before the Storm*, was produced in 1879, and his best-known work, *Effi Briest*, was written 16 years later at the age of 76. His output explored the workings of **high German society**; he was widely regarded as the first German author to document accurately both a society and an era.

Opposite: *Berlin covers the musical spectrum, from street performances to highbrow classical concerts.*
Left: *Memorials from pre-Prussian times abound throughout Berlin, to the greater good of the city.*

GERMAN WINE

Forget the ubiquitous **Liebfraumilch**: the majority of Berlin restaurants can offer a selection of quality German wines that will not have you clamouring for French or Italian. Most German wine is **white**, owing to a shortage of grape-ripening sunshine in northern latitudes, but a limited amount of **Rhine red** is produced. The **Rhine** and **Mosel** valleys are the chief producing areas, with the **Main River** in **Franconia** and **Baden** also contributing. Cheaper wines are classified as *Tafelwein* (table wine); popular varieties include Riesling, Traminer, Niersteiner Domtal, Piesporter and Oppenheimer. Note that Rhine wine comes in brown rather than green bottles.

In the 1920s, **Alfred Döblin's** (1878–1957) *Berlin Alexanderplatz* took the lid off the Berlin underworld in the days of the Weimar Republic, while around the same period dramatist and poet **Bertolt Brecht** (1898–1956) was producing the first of his works (*see* box, page 35). Under the Third Reich, the flow of literature all but dried up; the ceremonious book-burning by students and Nazi stormtroopers on Bebelplatz in May 1933 drove writers underground and production virtually ceased. It took leading West German novelist **Günter Grass** to settle in Berlin in the late 1950s – his satirical contribution of the time was *The Tin Drum* – for the city's literary fortunes to turn for the better. However, censorship prevailed in the eastern city and only in the GDR's latter days was there any relaxation by the authorities.

Food and Drink

The German capital is a veritable paradise for gourmets and snackers alike, with a profusion of restaurants, cafés, fast-food outlets and *Imbiss* street stalls. Since reunification, the eastern part of the city centre has spawned numerous new eating places, particularly in the **Oranienburger Straße** area and also **Prenzlauer Berg** – both are worthy alternatives to the much-favoured **Ku'damm** area of Charlottenburg.

Below: *The house of Bertolt Brecht at Chausseestraße 125 is a museum devoted to the dramatist.*

Breakfast in Berlin can be either the full hotel works or it can be a café blow-out – whichever option you choose, you will probably eat enough to last you for most of the day. Some Berlin cafés serve 'breakfast' until early afternoon – at the Café Bleibtreu in Bleibtreustraße, you can choose from at least half a dozen types of breakfast.

Lunch tends to be cheaper than **dinner**; for most Germans it is the main meal of the day. Both meals often start with **soup** – *Bohnensuppe* (bean soup), the Bavarian *Leberknödelsuppe* (a clear soup with liver-filled dumplings) and *Soljanke* (a spiced-up Ukranian soup) are favourites. Main courses are traditionally heavy, with **pork** a popular base: *Kassler Rippen* (smoked pork chops) and *Eisbein* (boiled pig's knuckle, usually served with pickled cabbage called *Sauerkraut*) are authentic Berlin dishes. Other pork-based dishes include all kinds of *Schnitzel*, *Schweinehaxe* (grilled pork knuckle) and *Schweinebraten* (roast pork), while **beef** and **chicken** are also available. Freshwater **fish** include *Zander* (pike-perch), *Aal* (eel) and *Forelle* (trout). **Vegetables** generally focus on potatoes – fried as in *Bratkartoffeln*, mashed, jacket or boiled –

and cabbage, often red and mixed with apple. Vegetarians, starved of decent vegetarian restaurants, could do worse than simply order a mixed salad; German **salads** are substantial and come served in their own dish. If you can find room, a typical German **dessert** is *Kompott* (stewed fruit).

Germany produces a fine range of **wines** (*see* box, opposite page), and restaurants will also list international labels, particularly from France, Italy and Spain. But the favourite alcoholic drink by far is **beer** – Germans down 140 litres (246 pints) per head each year and the choice is enormous. As well as the ubiquitous draught Pils, there is bottled light beer, dark beer, wheat beer, old beer and even fruit beer; *Berliner Weisse* (Berlin White) is a frothy wheat beer served in a large bowl-shaped glass and mixed with raspberry or green woodruff syrup. A winter tradition is to chase down the beer with a glass of *Schnaps*, a potent and warming distilled mix of alcohol and potato or fruits – mainly apricots, plums or cherries.

Above: *Hearty German fare washed down with a beer or two. Lunch is usually the main meal of the day and dishes are often rather heavy.*

SNACKING OUT

Germans are big **pork** eaters and are renowned for their varieties of **sausage** – try any *Imbiss* fast-food stand in the street for a *Bockwurst* (boiled sausage), *Bratwurst* (grilled sausage) or the Berlin speciality *Currywurst* (sausage with a rich curry sauce). Also popular are spicy **meatballs** called *Bouletten* and various types of **pizza** and **kebab**.

2
The Eastern City

Though the Wall and most reminders of it have long gone, Berlin's centre retains a double identity – the western part, with its parklands, palaces and prime shopping districts, and the eastern part which is undergoing large-scale regeneration after four depressed decades under the communists. The fusion between west and east has been slow, but has largely been accomplished.

UNTER DEN LINDEN

The wide boulevard stretching east from the Brandenburg Gate for 1.5km (0.75 miles) is Unter den Linden, laid down as a bridle route from the long demolished **Berliner Schloß** (palace) by the River Spree (*see* page 43) to the **Tiergarten**, its former hunting grounds. It takes its name from the lime, or linden, trees flanking the wide promenade that runs down the centre of the avenue – generally great to stroll down, but less so into the teeth of a biting easterly wind in mid-winter. With the Wall in place, this was the road to nowhere for the people of East Berlin: it ended just short of where the West began.

Brandenburg Gate ★★★

Previously the western entrance into the city, the Brandenburg Gate is the only survivor of the 18 gateways that once surrounded Berlin, and the symbol of its reunification. Built in 1791 to the plans of **Carl Gotthard Langhans**, the neoclassical gateway with its two rows of six Doric columns was styled on the Propylaea entrance to the Acropolis in Athens. The

DON'T MISS

★★★ **Brandenburg Gate:** 200-year-old symbol of Berlin.
★★★ **Unter den Linden:** fine buildings along Berlin's famous avenue.
★★★ **Gendarmenmarkt:** elegant early 18th-century square.
★★★ **Museums Island:** historical heart in more ways than one.
★★ **Bebelplatz:** site of the Nazis' book-burning in 1933.
★★ **German History Museum:** plenty to see in the former armoury.
★★ **Berliner Dom:** Berlin's turn-of-the-century cathedral.

Opposite: *Unter den Linden is one of Berlin's main thoroughfares.*

copper **Quadriga** statue – a winged Victory aboard her four-horse chariot – was the work of **Johann Gottfried Schadow** in 1794; in 1806 it was removed to Paris by the victorious Napoleon following his conquest of the Prussian army at Jena, but returned in 1814 by the Prussian Field Marshal Blücher.

Above: *The Brandenburg Gate is a former entrance to the city.*

Pariser Platz ★

The Brandenburg Gate sits astride the main west-east axis through central Berlin and facing east overlooks Pariser Platz, an attractive square that from 1735 was framed by Baroque town palaces. The palaces were destroyed in World War II and since reunification modern buildings have taken their place. On either side of the gateway, neo-classical mansions built in sandstone have gone some way in helping the square to recapture a measure of its former elegance. Here is the rebuilt luxury Hotel Adlon and nearby are the relocated British, French and American **embassies**.

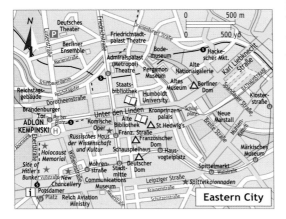

Holocaust Memorial ★★

The Memorial to the Murdered Jews of Europe, just south of the Brandeburg Gate, was inaugurated in May 2005, 60 years after the end of World War II. The grid of 2711 concrete slabs (the Field of Stelae) can be walked through from all sides; beneath it, the underground information centre provides background information on the Holocaust and its victims. Head in an easterly direction from Pariser Platz and two blocks further on the right you will find the mighty **Russian Embassy** in the Stalinist *Zuckerbäckerstil* ('wedding-cake' style) of the 1950s. A little further is the ticket office of the **Komische Oper**, which stages lighter operatic performances; the building itself is behind on Behrenstraße. On the corner of Charlottenstraße, the small Deutsche Guggenheim houses temporary exhibitions.

National Library **

A little further along Unter den Linden, beyond Friedrichstraße (*see* below), an archway on your left leads into the ivy-covered courtyard of the **Staatsbibliothek** (National Library). Commissioned by Kaiser Wilhelm II in 1903 and completed in 1914 as the Prussian State Library, it replaced the Baroque **Alte Bibliothek** (Old Library) – *see* Bebelplatz, page 35 – on the opposite side of the avenue; more recently it served as the GDR State Library. Behind its dark neo-Baroque façade there are some six million items, and today it is an information point for many of the 22,000 students at next-door **Humboldt University**.

The neoclassical university building was designed as a royal palace by Georg von Knobelsdorff for Prince Heinrich, brother of King Friedrich II (Frederick the Great), and completed in 1753; it became Berlin's first university in 1810 at the instigation of Prussian minister Wilhelm von Humboldt. The impressive bronze equestrian monument between the traffic lanes of Unter den Linden is of **Frederick the Great**. The creation of Christian Daniel Rauch in 1851, it was removed to Potsdam during World War II, but was returned to Berlin in 1980.

FRIEDRICHSTRAßE

Before World War II the meeting of Unter den Linden and Friedrichstraße was a hub of Berlin social life. Here, on the southwest corner directly opposite the now

TWO-WHEEL TAXI

Brandenburg Gate is a good point to hail one of the environmentally friendly bicycle rickshaws (**velotaxis**) now plying Berlin's streets as part of the city's transport network. Be transported along Unter den Linden to Alexanderplatz, through the Tiergarten to Zoologischer Garten or up to the Reichstag and around. Velotaxis hold two people; fares start at €2.50 or around €8 for 30 minutes of travel.

Below: *The entrance off Unter den Linden to the National Library courtyard.*

MAX REINHARDT

From the time Otto Brahm, director of Berlin's Deutsches Theater, gave the 21-year-old Max Reinhardt his stage break in 1894, the foundation was laid for the actor's subsequent career as a **theatre director**. He replaced Brahm at the Deutsches Theater in 1905 and founded the Volksbühne, **Berlin's People's Theatre**, in 1913. Through the 1920s and 1930s, the Jewish-born Reinhardt continued his work as a producer of innovative theatre in Berlin. With Germany under Nazi control in 1933, he returned to his native Austria. He moved to the USA in 1938 and died in New York in 1943.

demolished Hotel Unter den Linden, stood the famous **Café Kranzler**, now established on the Kurfürstendamm. Friedrichstraße, an important north-south axis through the city, has been given a facelift as the Mitte district's main shopping and entertainment centre, with Jean Nouvel's dramatic Galeries Lafayette building (Quartier 207) and the trendy Friedrichstadt-Passagen arcade (Quartier 206) designed by Henry Cobb, south of Unter den Linden, contributing to its revival. Step inside the Galeries Lafayette and marvel at the multistorey light-reflecting glass funnel around which the shopping floors are layered. Across the street, Russian culture lives on in the Russisches Haus der Wissenschaft und Kultur.

Three blocks north of Unter den Linden, past the towering glass Internationales Handelszentrum trade centre built by the GDR as a commercial showpiece to rival West Berlin in architectural design, is Friedrichstraße U-Bahn and S-Bahn station. Before 1990, it was the principal border-crossing point for travellers to

East Berlin; for East Berliners it was the end of the line. Outside the station until recently stood the **Tränenpalast** (Palace of Tears), the building through which Western visitors departed the East.

Theatre District ★★

Berlin's theatreland, immediately to the north of Friedrichstraße station, is fragmented and still being revived after years of neglect under the GDR. On the east side of Friedrichstraße is the **Admiralspalast** with its fine fluted columns and bas-reliefs. It was built in 1910 and now houses two theatres – the satirical cabaret **Die Distel** and, across an attractive inner courtyard, the Admiralspalast Theatre, given to staging lighter musical productions.

Left: *The attractive court-yard of the Admiralspalast Theatre.*

Opposite: *Shopping in the dramatically designed Galeries Lafayette can be quite an experience.*

To the north, on the opposite side of the River Spree and across a small park on Bertolt-Brecht-Platz, is the **Berliner Ensemble** theatre, with a rather austere exterior that does very little to enhance its run-down surroundings. Bertolt Brecht founded the theatre after his return from American exile and it celebrated its 50th anniversary as the official Brecht theatre in 1999; performances of the great man's work are staged regularly. In the park are a seated statue of Brecht and three marble pillars bearing his words.

The **Deutsches Theater** on nearby Schumannstraße was founded in 1883 and prospered under the direction of Otto Brahm from 1894 and under impressario Max Reinhardt from 1905 until 1932; busts of both men line the theatre's forecourt. This was where Marlene Dietrich made her stage debut in 1922; now the Deutsches Theater has a reputation second to none among Berlin theatres. Back on Friedrichstraße, the big and brash **Friedrichstadt-palast** revue theatre stages revue shows complete with full orchestra and chorus girls. North of here, close to Zinnowitzer Straße U-Bahn station, is the small **Fürst Oblomov Theatre** in a former factory building.

BEBELPLATZ

Fine buildings take up three sides of Bebelplatz – the Alte Bibliothek from 1781, the Deutsche Staatsoper (the National Opera House) and St Hedwig's Cathedral. But step into the middle of the square to review one of the most poignant episodes in the history of Berlin: here on the

BERTOLT BRECHT

The German **poet** and **dramatist** commemorated on Bertolt-Brecht-Platz in Mitte was born in 1898. His plays, which included *The Threepenny Opera*, for which Kurt Weill provided the music, *Mother Courage and her Children* and *The Caucasian Chalk Circle*, were experimental in nature, and characterized German drama in the period between the wars. Brecht, a fervent Marxist, had moved to Berlin in 1924; he left Germany for Russia when the Nazis came to power in 1933 and moved to the USA in 1941. He returned from exile after World War II and in 1949 founded the **Berliner Ensemble** theatre, which since his death in 1956 has continued to specialize in his work.

Above: *The clean architectural lines of the National Opera House on Bebelplatz.*
Opposite: *The design of Berlin's St Hedwig's Cathedral is reminiscent of the Pantheon in Rome.*

former Opernplatz on 10 May 1933, Josef Goebbels' young Nazis demonstrated their warped ideology by burning 20,000 books they claimed were lacking in German spirit. Among the authors whose works were destroyed were Thomas Mann, Kurt Tucholsky and Heinrich Heine, along with the dramatist Bertolt Brecht. A window in the cobbled square looks down on to empty shelves and Heine's prophetic words of 1820 are recalled: 'Where they start by burning books, they'll finish by burning people.'

Old Library ★★

Along the right side of Bebelplatz is the pleasing curved Baroque façade of the restored **Alte Bibliothek** – it was the only part of the building to survive the war. The former royal library, built between 1775 and 1780, it has long worn the humorous tag 'die Kommode' (chest of drawers) given to it by locals. The building is now part of Humboldt University, which is located directly across Unter den Linden.

National Opera House ★★

Facing the Alte Bibliothek on Bebelplatz, the **Deutsche Staatsoper** was Berlin's very first theatre and also the first building on what subsequently became known as the Forum Fridericianum. Designed by leading Berlin architect Georg von Knobelsdorff, it was completed in 1743. The Staatsoper was also the first important Berlin building to suffer serious wartime damage when it was bombed on the night of 9–10 April 1941; though the Nazis restored the theatre for its bicentenary two years later, it was hit again in 1945 and not rebuilt a second time until as late as the 1950s. With its neoclassical gabled portico supported by six Corinthian columns, very much in the Von Knobelsdorff style, the clean-lined Staatsoper presents a

ROUTE 100

Every city has its favoured bus route – Berlin's is Route 100, which cuts a swath right through the city centre and takes in many of the major sights. The double-decker service runs from **Zoologischer Garten** station at the end of the **Ku'damm** in the western city centre via the **Brandenburg Gate**, **Reichstag** and **Unter den Linden** to **Alexanderplatz** in the eastern part. For the cost of a single ticket you can climb on and off as many times as you like within two hours of boarding; if you stay on the bus the trip takes about 45 minutes.

pleasing architectural balance with the Alte Bibliothek.

The southeast corner of Bebelplatz is occupied by the copper-domed **St Hedwig's Cathedral** of 1747, its design by Von Knobelsdorff based on the Pantheon in Rome. Friedrich II ordered a church to be built to appease the Catholic minority incorporated into protestant Prussia after his successful Silesia campaign – it has been a cathedral since 1929. The building's modern interior was created in 1963; an eminent worshipper on 23 June 1996 was Pope John Paul II.

Crown Princes' Palace *

Beyond Bebelplatz is the newly restored **Kronprinzen-palais**, dating from 1663 and restyled in the Baroque style in 1732 for the future King Friedrich II; it is linked to the Opernpalais by an arched bridge. It was a royal residence until the end of World War I and subsequently accommodated important visitors to the city in GDR days. It now houses temporary exhibitions. Next door, the Opernpalais or Crown Princesses' Palace (**Kronprinzessinenpalais**), now housing the Operncafé, was the princesses' Baroque town house; it was restored in 1964 after World War II destruction.

New Guardhouse *

Opposite the Kronprinzessinenpalais on Unter den Linden, the former royal guardhouse, or **Neue Wache**, was built by Schinkel in 1818 for King Friedrich Wilhelm III. It served as a World War I memorial from 1931 and became the GDR's monument to the victims of fascism and militarism from 1957 until 1989. In GDR times there was an hourly changing of the guard by goose-stepping soldiers. The Neue Wache underwent extensive reconstruction in 1998 and today houses a much-enlarged version of Käthe Kollwitz's sculpture of a mother with her dead son.

SUPREME ARCHITECT

The architect **Georg von Knobelsdorff** (1699–1753), a friend of Frederick the Great, was a key figure in the transition from Baroque to neoclassical building design. A student of the court painter **Antoine Pesne**, he reached a peak in the 1740s, helping to plan Frederick the Great's **Forum Fridericianum** on the site of present-day Bebelplatz, and designing the **National Opera House** there. In 1747 he designed what many regard as his masterpiece, the **Schloß Sanssouci** at Potsdam. Another of his palatial creations was the **Schloß Rheinsberg**, 90km (56 miles) north of Berlin.

STROLL THE STREETS

While many of Berlin's main sights can be seen from the comfort of an air-conditioned tour bus, by far the best way to discover the city is on foot. Regular **guided walks** take place throughout the city, each dwelling on a particular theme, with titles such as: 'Hidden Berlin', 'Third Reich Berlin', 'Behind The Iron Curtain' and 'The New Jewish Berlin'. The walks and tours by bike have become popular with residents and visitors alike – the **Berlin Tourist Office** can help with details.

Above: *Soldiers once goose-stepped before the New Guardhouse on Unter den Linden.*
Opposite: *The neo-classical German Cathedral looks out over the Gendarmenmarkt.*
Below: *The German History Museum is housed in a former armoury.*

German History Museum ★★
Beyond the Neue Wache is the **Deutsches Historisches Museum**, housed in the faded pink Baroque Zeughaus, the former Prussian armoury building of 1695–1706. The architects included Johann Nering and Andreas Schlüter, whose 22 death masks of warriors are on display in the covered inner courtyard. The museum, which plots Germany's history in paintings, documentaries and films, reopened in 2005 after a major reconstruction that included the addition of the glass I. M. Pau Building for housing temporary exhibitions. It is open daily 10:00–18:00. Tucked away behind the Zeughaus at Am Festungsgraben is the **Maxim Gorki Theatre**, which since 1995 has staged contemporary productions and selective works by Russian playwrights.

GENDARMENMARKT
A few minutes' walk south of Unter den Linden, situated among the streets of Friedrichstadt, is the cobbled Gendarmenmarkt, with its theatre and its twin cathedrals that were beautifully restored after their World War II destruction. The square, arguably one of the finest in Berlin, was the

brainchild of **King Friedrich I** and resumed its earlier identity in the 1990s, having been called Platz der Akademie under the GDR. Its present name is derived from the Gendarme regiment which had its headquarters there in the mid-1700s. Nowadays the Gendarmenmarkt and the streets in the immediate vicinity sport a number of high-class restaurants that have given the whole area a new identity.

The Two Cathedrals **

At either end of the square, and striking neoclassical architectural harmony with the solid Schauspielhaus between them, are the German cathedral (Deutscher Dom) and French cathedral (Französischer Dom). Only the French cathedral, at the square's northern end, has been used recently for religious services; the German cathedral houses the historical exhibition 'Milestones, Setbacks, Sidetracks – The Path to Parliamentary Democracy in Germany', on five floors, from the effects of the French Revolution in 1789 to unification in 1990. It is open Tuesday–Sunday 10:00–18:00 (May–September 10:00–19:00), and entrance is free.

The **Französischer Dom** was completed in 1705 as the church of the French Huguenots, who had fled to Berlin to escape persecution two decades earlier. It was designed on the lines of the Huguenots' own church in Charenton, with the dome by Karl von Gontard added in 1785. Today the Huguenot Museum, tracing their history in France and relocation to Berlin and Brandenburg, and the Huguenot Library occupy part of the building; the church was reconsecrated in 1983 after a lengthy period of restoration. The museum is open Tuesday–Saturday 12:00–17:00, Sunday 11:00–17:00.

The **Deutscher Dom** was completed in 1708, three years later, for Lutherans living in Berlin and in 1785 it also added a Karl von Gontard dome supported by

SCHILLER'S STAGE

Friedrich Schiller, whose statue occupies a prominent position on Gendarmenmarkt, was born in 1759 and started his working life as a **military surgeon**, but altered course and established himself as one of Germany's leading 18th-century **dramatists**. He had a major hit with his revolutionary-themed *The Robbers* in 1782, and also wrote *Ode to Joy, Don Carlos, The Maid of Orleans* and *William Tell*. He completed a history of the Thirty Years' War at Jena before moving to Weimar, where he died in 1805.

Right: *The Berlin Concert Hall and French Cathedral co-exist in harmony.*
Opposite: *The mighty Pergamon Museum.*

STALL FOR TIME

If you enjoy ferreting around market stalls for old *objets d'art*, the following venues will appeal:
• The **Big Berlin Junk and Art Market**, Berlin's biggest and most popular art and flea market, held on Straße des 17 Juni on Saturday and Sunday (11:00–19:00).
• The **Flohmarkt** (Flea Market) **am Mauerpark**, by a surviving section of the Berlin Wall in Prenzlauer Berg, is a recent addition. It's on Sundays (08:00–18:00).
• The **Trödelmarkt am Rathaus Schöneberg** (by Schöneberg Town Hall), site of John F. Kennedy's famous speech, is popular with locals. It's on Saturday and Sunday (08:00–16:00).
• A second-hand **book mart** is held from time to time outside Humboldt University on Unter den Linden.

Corinthian columns. The two cathedrals form a mirror image across the square, at one time the setting for a bustling market; now tourists pace the square seeking the best photographic angle.

Berlin Concert Hall ★★

Along the western side of Gendarmenmarkt is the massive Berlin Concert Hall, formerly the theatre or Schauspielhaus. The building was designed by **Karl Friedrich Schinkel** and it was completed in 1821 on the site of Carl Gotthard Langhans' creation that burned to the ground in 1817. Schinkel salvaged the six columns as well as stone from the original; though the theatre suffered severe war damage, it was fully restored in 1984 to be used as the city's prime concert venue, seating 1850 patrons, and is home to the Konzerthausorchester Berlin, formerly the **Berlin Symphony Orchestra**. In front of the building is a splended white marble statue of the great German dramatist and romantic poet **Friedrich Schiller** (*see* box, page 39), by Reinhold Begas.

MUSEUMS ISLAND

This is the cultural heart of Berlin, and the museums grouped on an island in the River Spree are a rich source of information for historian and casual visitor alike. The five museums were built between 1830 and 1930 – first to open was the Altes Museum, followed by the Neues Museum in 1855, Alte Nationalgalerie in 1876, Bodemuseum in 1904 and Pergamon Museum in 1930.

The **Altes Museum** (Old Museum), a masterpiece in neoclassicism, is generally held to be Germany's oldest museum. It was purpose-built by Karl Friedrich Schinkel and reopened in 1966 following postwar restoration. The main exhibition area houses Greek and Roman antiquities; here, too, is the Ägyptisches Museum (Egyptian Museum) and Papyrus Collection, relocated from Charlottenburg. Its well-known works include the bust of Queen Nefertiti and pieces from the time of King Akhenaton, around 1340BC from Tell El Amarna. In front of the Altes Museum is the **Lustgarten** (Pleasure Garden), a parade ground for King Friedrich Wilhelm I.

The distinctive **Alte Nationalgalerie** building, by Friedrich August Stüler, resembles a Corinthian temple atop a raised plinth, reached by a fine twin staircase. It contains 19th-century art from the French Revolution to World War I. Two rooms are devoted to Romanticism, highlighting the work of Caspar David Friedrich, while the second floor houses a rich Impressionist collection featuring Manet, Monet, Renoir, Degas and Cézanne. There is also a collection of works by Max Liebermann.

The reopening in October 2006 of the rebuilt neo-Baroque **Bodemuseum**, at the northern tip of Museums Island, brought together the Sculpture Collection and Museum of Byzantine Art, the latter focusing on the art of the western Roman and Byzantine empires. The **Neues Museum**, currently

MUSEUM ENTRY

A one-day or three-day ticket gives unrestricted entry to all museums and exhibitions run by Berlin State Museums (SMB). They include the **Altes Museum**, **Bodemuseum** and **Pergamon Museum** on Museums Island; the **Museum of Contemporary Art** at Hamburger Bahnhof; **Handicrafts Museum** and **New National Gallery** at Tiergarten; and **Ethnological Museum** and **Museum of European Cultures** at Dahlem. Entry is free to all SMB museums for four hours before closing on Thursdays. More information is available on the museum hotline: 20 90 55 55.

being rebuilt, is due to open in 2008 and will house collections from the Egyptian Museum and Museum of Primeval and Early History.

Largest of them all is the **Pergamon Museum**, which took 20 years to build from its foundation in 1910 to the design of Alfred Messel. Highlight of its classical antiquities collection is the three-storey-high Pergamon Altar, which stood at Pergamon in Asia Minor in 165BC. Other rooms contain good collections of Middle Eastern antiquities and Islamic art. The museums on Museums Island are open daily 10:00–18:00 (Thursday 10:00–22:00).

Berliner Dom **

Near the museums is Berlin's neo-Baroque cathedral, high church of Prussian Protestantism that was completed in 1905 and was the third place of worship on the site. The first Dominican Church, from 1297, was demolished in 1747 to make way for the cathedral of Georg von Knobelsdorff and Johann Boumann; in 1894, **Kaiser Wilhelm II** laid the foundation stone for the present neo-Renaissance style building – it was 12 years in the making. The cathedral suffered great wartime damage and its extensive restoration was completed only in 1993. Climb the 267 steps to the **Dome Gallery** – the dome is reminiscent of St Peter's in Rome – and descend to the well-lit crypt, where the sarcophagi of 95 Hohenzollerns are interred.

ASIAN ART

The **Museum für Asiatische Kunst** (Museum of Asian Art) in the Dahlem Complex at Lansstraße 8 in Zehlendorf includes the following:
• the **Museum für Indische Kunst** (Museum of Indian Art). Highlights include stone and bronze sculptures, terracotta work and miniatures from Pakistan, Afghanistan, Sri Lanka, India, Nepal, Tibet and Southeast Asia from the 2nd century BC to the present day.
• the **Museum für Ostasiatische Kunst** (Museum of East Asian Art). It features 4000 years of art and crafts from China, Japan and Korea from the early stone age to the present day in separate galleries, as well as Chinese and Japanese paintings, calligraphy, tea services and sculptures – and even a 17th-century Chinese imperial throne.

SCHLOßPLATZ

At the end of Unter den Linden, the Schloßbrücke leads ahead to the wide expanse of Schloßplatz, known as Marx-Engels-Platz in GDR times, where a large excavation site reveals the foundations of the splendid Royal Palace, the **Berliner Schloß**. The building, far more fortress than palace, was for years the seat of the Hohenzollern dynasty of Prussian kings and German emperors. Construction started in 1443 and over the years it took on a Renaissance guise; it was given its Baroque appearance by architect Andreas Schlüter and his successor Johann Friedrich Eosander. From its balcony, Karl Liebknecht proclaimed the German Socialist Republic in November 1918.

The castle suffered bomb damage on 3 February 1945, but was not beyond repair and immediately after the war it was still in use as a museum. However, in late 1950 Socialist Unity Party secretary Walter Ulbricht ordered the building to be dynamited. Grandiose long-term plans to rebuild the Berliner Schloß are now in hand.

Along the southern edge of Schloßplatz is the **State Council Building** from the early 1960s. Incorporated in the building is the Berliner Schloß balcony from which Karl Liebknecht proclaimed a socialist republic in 1918 following the Kaiser's abdication (*see* above). The building is now the Berlin Campus of the European School of Management and Technology, having served as the German Chancellor's temporary office post-reunification. Across Breite Straße, to the east, are the New Royal Stables (**Neue Marstall**), an unimpressive early 20th-century building which housed the royal livery from the turn of the century and are now a repository for Berlin's city archives.

Above: *The Palace of the Republic before its demolition in 2007.*
Opposite: *The magnificent Berliner Dom was built over a period of 12 years.*

ERICH'S SHOWPIECE

The **Palace of the Republic**, with its copper-tinted windows overlooking Schloßplatz, for long remained the largest relic of the German Democratic Republic still standing in Berlin. Dating from the early 1970s, it was the pride and joy of GDR leader **Erich Honecker** and was home to the state's *Volkskammer* parliament; it also contained a massive congress hall, as well as bars, restaurants and a bowling alley. Around the time of unification, in October 1990, asbestos was discovered in the building and it was immediately abandoned. Demolition of the building got under way in 2007.

LEIPZIGER STRAßE

Running parallel with Unter den Linden a few blocks to the south, Leipziger Straße was before the war one of Berlin's main shopping streets, linking Berlin's two great squares of Potsdamer Platz (see page 76) and Alexanderplatz (see page 54). Around the turn of the century it was still a peaceful residential quarter; now several huge 1970s GDR-built apartment blocks are strung out along its southern side and the ever-present sound of the traffic hastening its way along the twin carriageway means it is anything but quiet. Just south of here ran the Wall, and the development of the territory it occupied was far slower than elsewhere in Berlin.

Close to the western end of Leipziger Straße, before it reaches the massively redeveloped area around Potsdamer Platz, is the site of the **New Chancellery**. Built in 1938 and housing Hitler's office, it stood at the junction of Wilhelmstraße and Voss Straße, close to the present Mohrenstraße U-Bahn station. An apartment block and kindergarten are now on the site. A short distance to the west stood the **Old Chancellery**, in what for 28 years was the 'no-man's-land' of the Wall. Its garden contained **Hitler's bunker**, where the Führer spent the last six weeks of his life before committing suicide on 30 April 1945, blaming the German people for his failure to conquer Europe. Along Wilhelmstraße south of Leipziger Straße stands the huge building of the **Reich Aviation Ministry** that was headed by Hermann Göring. A survivor of the war, it became the GDR's first government headquarters and now houses the Federal Finance Ministry.

STREET PARTIES

Carnival has never really found its way to Berlin and the traditional carnival day (**Rosenmontag**, the Monday before Lent) is a normal working day in the capital. But Berlin nevertheless sports some lively summer street happenings. Look out for news of the **Love Parade**, the colourful **Carnival of Cultures**, the gay community's **Christopher Street Day Parade** and the *Fête de la Musique*.

Communications Museum ★

On Leipziger Straße, at the junction with Mauerstraße, the **Museum für Kommunikation Berlin** recalls the history of the post office in Prussia and the postal and tele-communications history of Berlin since the introduction of the postage stamp. Highlights include the highly prized blue twopenny Mauritius stamp and three talking robots. There are various changing exhibitions. Open Tuesday–Friday 09:00–17:00, Saturday–Sunday 11:00–19:00.

On the right along Leipziger Straße towards Spittel-markt is the semicircular **Spittelkolonnaden**, replicating part of a building that once stood nearby. The milestone in front of it is also a copy; both are dwarfed by the high-rise apartment blocks that provided high-density inner-city accommodation for East Berlin's population.

Märkisches Museum ★

From Spittelmarkt, Wallstraße leads parallel with the Spree canal to the red-brick Märkisches Museum, built between 1899 and 1908 to the design of Ludwig Hoffmann. The museum is dedicated to the history, art and culture of Berlin, with special sections that cover the theatre, design, literature and music. A highlight of the collection is the **automatophones**, mechanical musical intruments from the 18th century demonstrated on Sundays at 15:00. The museum is open Tuesday–Sunday 10:00–18:00 (Wednesday 12:00–20:00).

REICH REFLECTIONS

Berlin's streets and buildings today still reflect the style of the Nazi dictatorship. Look out for:
• the **street lanterns** selected by Hitler for Berlin's west-east axis road between Theodor-Heuss-Platz (formerly Adolf-Hitler-Platz) and the Brandenburg Gate;
• the **Olympic Stadium**, set-ting for the 1936 Olympic Games and newly rebuilt;
• the former **Reich Aviation Ministry** at the meeting of Leipziger Straße and Wilhelmstraße, now the Ministry of Finance;
• the former **Reichsbank** building at Werderscher Markt in Mitte, converted for use by the German Foreign Office.

Opposite: *Massive apart-ment blocks on Leipziger Straße overshadow the milestone and the ornate Spittelkolonnaden.*
Left: *The newly rebuilt Olympic Stadium staged the 2006 World Cup football final.*

3
Beyond the Spree

The River Spree, on which Berlin sits, flows from the **Fürstenwalder Forest** southeast of the city into the **Grosser Müggelsee**, the capital's largest lake, and then bisects the eastern city centre before meandering off in a northwesterly direction towards the lakes of Spandau. Unlike the days when the city was divided, pleasure cruises now operate around Berlin's historic centre and out to the new Spreebogen government quarter. They also extend way out into the suburbs – to Treptow, Spandau and Wannsee, also to Pfaueninsel and Potsdam.

Cross the **Liebknecht Brücke** over the Spree beyond the Berliner Dom and you are in the commercial centre of eastern Berlin. To your left is the Radisson SAS Hotel and the DomAquarée complex with its £8 million AquaDom, a 25-metre-high cylindrical glass fish tank right in the hotel lobby. A lift rises through the middle of the tank, home to 2600 fish of 56 species. To your right are the revived quarter of the Nikolaiviertel (see page 50) and the distinctive Red Town Hall. Straight ahead you cannot miss the TV Tower that dominates the Berlin skyline for miles around.

UNDER THE TV TOWER
Berlin City Hall ★
Across the wide expanse of Schloßplatz is the red-brick **Berliner Rathaus** (Berlin City Hall), formerly known as the Rotes Rathaus, or Red Town Hall, because of its colour rather than the political leanings of its administrators. It was built between 1861 and 1869 on the site of

BERLIN

DON'T MISS

*** Nikolaiviertel: cobblestone village-like quarter by the River Spree.
** Marienkirche: Berlin's oldest parish church.
** TV Tower: never fear – at 365m (1198ft) high you cannot miss it.
** Hackesche Höfe: restored Art Deco courtyards with small shops.
** Oranienburger Straße: emerging area for wining and dining.
* Alexanderplatz: it is not beautiful, but it is the hub of eastern Berlin.

Opposite: *A pleasure boat on the Spree passes the TV Tower and Berlin City Hall.*

VIEWS OF BERLIN

The best views of Berlin are to be had from the **Fernsehturm** (TV Tower) in the eastern city centre and the **Funkturm** (Radio Tower) at the Berlin Exhibition Grounds to the west. From the viewing gallery 200m (656ft) up the Fernsehturm (it translates as 'far-seeing tower'), on a clear day you can see 35km (22 miles) to the **countryside** beyond Berlin's borders. Closer to the tower you can identify the inner-city districts of Kreuzberg, Prenzlauer Berg and Friedrichshain. From the viewing gallery 130m (427ft) up the Funkturm there is a grand panorama of Berlin's **lake district** to the west of the city.

Opposite: *The contrasting styles of the TV Tower and tiny Marienkirche.*
Below: *Berlin's City Hall was once known as the Red Town Hall.*

Berlin's first 13th-century town hall and restored after suffering war damage; now it is the seat of the city's governing mayor and Berlin Senate. The neo-Renaissance design of Heinrich Friedrich Waesemann is typically north German; an interesting feature is the terracotta frieze depicting Berlin's history that was added in 1879. Open Monday–Friday 09:00–18:00. On the square in front of the City Hall is the **Neptunbrunnen** (Neptune's Fountain) of Reinhold Begas from 1891, with its four female figures representing the great rivers of Germany – the Rhine, Oder, Elbe and Weichsel.

Marienkirche ★★

The attractive little church that, like its surrounds, sits dwarfed by the TV Tower and looks strangely out of place set at an angle to Karl Liebknecht Straße on the vast pedestrian plaza, is the oldest parish church in Berlin. The nave dates from around 1270, though the lantern tower was a much later creation, the work of Carl Gotthard Langhans in 1790. The Baroque canopied **marble pulpit** of 1703 is attributed to Andreas Schlüter, and the large **bronze font** dates from the late 15th century. The 22m (72ft) medieval **frieze** is entitled *Totentanz* (Dance of Death).

TV Tower ★★

The 365m (1198ft) **Fernsehturm** (TV Tower), built in 1969, boasts the same quality as the reviled Palace of Culture in Warsaw. The most widely held opinion in Berlin is that the best view of the city is the view from the top of the TV Tower, because that is the only place from which you cannot see the structure itself. On a clear day take the fast elevator

to the viewing gallery; afterwards, you can enjoy a cold beer or a cup of coffee in the slowly revolving **Telecafé**. More than 1.2 million visitors get upwardly mobile each year; the tower is open daily from 09:00–24:00 March to October and 10:00–24:00 November to February. At the base of the tower, quite a lot needs to be done to the windswept concrete surrounds to make the area appealing.

The hefty bronze **Marx-Engels statue** by Ludwig Engelhardt that sits in the former Marx Engels Forum is a rather poignant reflection on the 40 years of GDR history. The founders of communism, Karl Marx and Friedrich Engels, gaze upon a part of the city that has long turned its back on their tried, tested and failed philosophies.

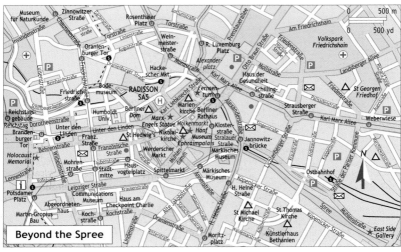

Beyond the Spree

Above: *Attractive cafés line the bank of the Spree in the Nikolaiviertel.*

HITLER'S DREAM

Hitler's vision of the new **Germania**, as Berlin was to have been called, involved a grand-scale plan for the city centre. A new north-south **axis road** 7km (4 miles) long was to have cut right through the heart of the city, lined with palatial government buildings; at either end of this super highway, Hitler's chief architect **Albert Speer** had planned massive towers holding over 150,000 people. The grandiose scheme was quickly forgotten after the onset of World War II.

NIKOLAIVIERTEL

The traffic thunders by on the Mühlendamm, but inside the **Nikolaiviertel** (Nikolai Quarter) nothing stirs, save for the small groups of tourists shuffling up and down the narrow cobbled streets and alleyways and drifting in and out of the little cluster of shops, boutiques, restaurants and cafés.

The rebuilding of Berlin's war-damaged medieval quarter was a surprising piece of initiative by the GDR government to celebrate the 750th anniversary of the city and restore character to an area that had been flattened in 1944. Some buildings are faithful reconstructions of those that failed to survive the war – like the copy of the 16th-century tavern **Zum Nussbaum** (At The Nut Tree), now housing a popular restaurant – the original stood on nearby Fischerinsel and was said to be a favourite watering hole of cartoonist Heinrich Zille. Others were imaginatively built in the style of the time; all are constructed out of the same prefabricated concrete blocks that went into most GDR buildings. Nowadays a village-like atmosphere prevails in this part of town and it is hard to believe that just across Spandauer Straße is the City Hall and beyond it busy Alexanderplatz.

Nikolaikirche ★★

The distinctive twin-spired parish church of St Nicholas that gives its name to the area is one of the oldest in Berlin, having been restored rather than rebuilt from scratch. Its origins date from the 13th century, though the present Gothic-styled building was finished in 1470. The church has great historical significance for Berlin, for here in 1307 the towns of Berlin and Cölln were officially joined. Rarely used for services nowadays, it houses exhibitions from the **Märkisches Museum** (*see* page 45) and other Berlin museums. There are some religious **sculptures**, including the *Spandauer Madonna* from 1290. The church is open Tuesday–Sunday 10:00–18:00.

Ephraimpalais ★

When the first Ephraimpalais was knocked down to make way for the Mühlendamm bridge over the Spree in 1935, its splendid **curved façade** was taken down piece by piece and stored in the western part of the city. The façade was returned to East Berlin in 1984 to be incorporated into the Nikolaiviertel project; now the Rococo building, with its golden-painted **balconies** and stone **cherubs**, is regarded as one of the most attractive in Berlin and is used for rotating art and history exhibitions. The original mansion house was built between 1761 and 1765 for the court jeweller and banker Veitel Ephraim. Open Tuesday–Sunday 10:00–18:00 (Wednesday 12:00–20:00).

Knoblauchhaus ★

Besides the Nikolaikirche, the stuccoed Knoblauchhaus in Poststraße, once owned by the Knoblauch family (the family name means 'garlic'), is the Nikolaiviertel's only genuine old building. Designed by **Friedrich Wilhelm Dietrichs**, it was completed in 1759 and amazingly survived World War II. The building is open to the public and shows the lifestyle of a well-off 19th-century Berlin family, complete with art works and period Biedermeier furniture.

Hanf Museum ★

On the fringe of the Nikolaiviertel, at Mühlendamm 5, the Hanf Museum (Hemp Museum) that opened in 1994 tells the history of **hemp cultivation** and its use in medicine, agriculture and building – also its cultural and religious uses and the legal implications of the controversial plant. There's a café where you can sample cakes made with hemp. Plenty of information, too, some of it in English. Open Tuesday–Friday 10:00–20:00, Saturday–Sunday 12:00–20:00.

TIPPING

Though **restaurants** usually include a **service charge**, it is customary to increase the amount by 5–10 per cent to the nearest round total. For example, if the restaurant bill comes to €38.50, expect to hand over €40. For **taxi drivers**, the recommended tip is the universal 10 per cent and it is usual to give **porters** and **cloakroom attendants** 50c to €1. A consideration of between €2–€4, depending on the duration of the tour, is apprecated by **tour guides**.

Below: *The distinctive twin spires of the restored Nikolaikirche.*

KEEP A LATE DATE

Berlin's nightlife keeps late
hours. **Clubs** rarely get going
much before 22:00 and can be
pretty quiet until midnight. As
there are no licensing hours,
some places do not even open
until midnight and have no set
hours – they keep going until
dawn or later. The club scene
is ever changing, so refer to an
updated listing to find out
what is happening and where.
Familiarize yourself with the
comprehensive **night bus**
scene, and remember you can
always take the first **U-Bahn**
'home' at around 04:30.

AROUND MOLKENMARKT

The Mühlendamm leads on to Molkenmarkt (Milk Market),
in medieval times Berlin's busiest marketplace, but you
wouldn't think so now – it is one of the noisiest inter-
sections. Along its southern side by the river is the mint
building or **Reichsmünze**, built in the mid-1930s and bearing a copy of the frieze designed by Gottfried Schadow for
the first Berlin mint. Incorporated in the complex –
together the buildings made up the former GDR Ministry
of Culture – is the 18th-century **Palais Schwerin**, built for
Otto Schwerin, a minister at the time of Friedrich I.

The bulk of the red-brick City Hall lies just to the north;
to the right is the domed tower of the **Alte Stadthaus** (Old
Town Hall) which, despite its older appearance, was built
at the start of the 1900s for the Berlin authorities. It was
used by the GDR ministers' council pre-1989 and has just
been fully refurbished.

The area around Judenstraße once housed Berlin's
Jewish community; down Parochialstraße at the end on
Klosterstraße is the late 17th-century Baroque **Parochial-
kirche** of Johann Arnold Nering. It was bombed in the war
and underwent a complete restoration between 1987 and
2003. North on the same side of Klosterstraße you cannot
miss the **Palais Podewil**, a former manor house from 1704
that has been successfully converted into an arts and
drama centre and now stages film, drama, dance and concert performances.

TRABBIES LIVE ON

They sound like a motorized
lawn mower; they are
powered by a two-stroke
500cc engine that pushes
great clouds of blue smoke
into the atmosphere. As the
people's car of the GDR, the
little two-door **Trabant** with its
fibreglass body was produced
by the thousand – every third
car on the road was a Trabant.
Now visitors to Berlin can
drive their own 'trabi' on one
of the two routes with Trabi
Safari – 'Classic' or 'Wild
East'. A guide accompanies
tours, providing explanations
by radio – English is available
with advance notice. Tel:
2759 2273. The trip lasts 90
minutes and costs €25–€35.

Left: *The Franziskaner Klosterkirche is a haven of peace in the city centre.*
Opposite: *The ubiquitous little Trabant was the people's car of the former East Germany.*
Below: *The distinctive neo-Baroque frontage of the Stadtgericht, Berlin's attractive Courthouse.*

Franziskaner Klosterkirche ★

Towards the looming TV Tower, the ruin on the right of Klosterstraße is the red-brick Franziskaner Klosterkirche (Franciscan Abbey Church), with origins going back to the 13th century. Iron gates lead to the three-nave interior, a place of tranquility that is open to the sky and surrounded by greenery and birdsong. The church was blown up by a land mine in 1945.

Courthouse ★

A walk through the gardens to the right of the ruined church brings you on to Littenstraße. Almost directly opposite is the rounded neo-Baroque exterior of the **Stadtgericht** (Courthouse) – step inside to see Berlin's finest *Jugendstil* (Art Nouveau) staircases that weave their way down through the centre of the building. Head south and into Waisenstraße for a drink in Berlin's oldest pub, the endearingly named **Zur Letzten Instanz** (Last Appeal Court). The building dates from 1621 – the inn's name alludes to the judicial building up the street; perhaps it was a place for the drowning of sorrows? A section of Berlin's first **wall** stands preserved nearby – not the 4m (14ft) monstrosity that bisected the city in the Cold War days, but the fortification that surrounded the city from the 13th century.

ALEXANDERPLATZ

When the winter wind blows cold in the western part of Berlin, it fairly whistles across Alexanderplatz, the vast open square that forms a hub of the eastern city centre. It is a bleak and soulless place of concrete, tiles and tarmac, surrounded by austere **GDR architecture** of the 1960s – if ever a place needed pulling to bits and starting again, this is it. In some ways it was better in GDR days, without the gaudy neon signs that now surmount most buildings around the square; there is even a flickering video screen atop one building, pumping out its unwatched commercials over the heads of the scurrying masses.

The square the locals call 'Alex' was renamed from **Ochsenmarkt** (Oxen Market) to mark the visit of the Russian Czar **Alexander I** to Berlin in 1805. It achieved fame with the publication of Alfred Döblin's novel *Berlin Alexanderplatz* in the late 1920s, by which time its fine turn-of-the-century reputation as a prime shopping and nightlife centre had all but faded. Severely bombed in World War II, the square was given its current appearance by uninspired GDR architects in the 1960s; a master plan by Berlin architect **Hans Kollhoff** for the square's redevelopment is still under consideration.

Alexanderplatz has always been a **transport** hub; Berlin's first U-Bahn (underground) station opened here in 1913, while from the S-Bahn (suburban) station trains run every couple of minutes to Friedrichstraße, Hauptbahnhof and Zoologischer Garten – other key S-Bahn stations. An extension to eastern Berlin's tram network now bisects the square

---

GOING UNDERGROUND

Berlin's **U-Bahn** underground railway system is clean and efficient, with trains operating at frequent intervals over 10 lines. **Stations** are identified at street level by a white 'U' on a blue background; trains run from 05:00–00:30, with lines U9 and U12 operating round the clock at weekends. In an overall expansion of Berlin's city transportation, more lines are being added, particularly serving outlying areas in the north of the city. The network connects with the 14 lines of the **S-Bahn** (suburban) network.

and the presence of bright yellow trams at least adds a splash of colour to the drab surrounds. Before the lines were laid, grassy banks and flower beds were put down on top of the tiles in an imaginative effort to colour the place up.

The tallest building on Alexanderplatz is the **Park Inn**, Berlin's largest hotel by far with 1012 guest rooms and a 37th-floor casino. A legacy of the GDR's 'big is beautiful' building philosophy, it was initially the Hotel Stadt Berlin and then part of the Forum chain.

There are two landmarks on Alexanderplatz – the **Weltzeituhr** (World Clock), showing the time in cities throughout the world, and the **Brunnen der Völkerfreundschaft** (People's Friendship Fountain) in front of the Kaufhof department store.

The pedestrian way into Alexanderplatz from Rathausstraße, at the square's southern corner, passes between two early eight-storey 1930s buildings designed by Peter Behrens, the **Alexanderhaus** and **Berolinahaus** – the only buildings on Alexanderplatz left standing at the end of the war. The Alexanderhaus now houses the head-quarters of the Landesbank Berlin and a small shopping mall, while the Berolinahaus, a protected monument that had been empty since 1998, now has a C&A clothing store occupying four floors.

'ALEX' ON HIGH

By the time you read this, there is a remote chance that work may have begun on a bold development entitled '**Ten Skyscrapers at the Alex**' that is intended to transform Alexanderplatz and the immediate area. An outline date of 2010 was initially set for completion of the project, which was conceived at the end of the 1990s. Architects **Hans Kollhoff**, **Jürgen Sawade** and **Christoph Ingenhoven** were commis-sioned to produce a new look for the huge largely pedestri-anized square and came up with a futuristic design based on 10 high-rise buildings. It is a controversial proposal that may or may not happen.

Opposite: *The World Clock on Alexanderplatz keeps Berliners informed of the time around the world.*
Left: *The People's Friendship Fountain is another well-known land-mark on the wide open eastern city square.*

THE DISTRICTS

Berlin's **23 administrative districts** have been reduced to a more manageable 12 boroughs by pairing up some of the districts.
• The **inner districts** comprise Charlottenburg, Mitte, Friedrichshain, Kreuzberg, Prenzlauer Berg, Schöneberg, Tiergarten and Wedding.
• Districts in the **outer ring** are (in clockwise order) Wilmersdorf, Spandau, Reinickendorf, Pankow, Weissensee, Hohenschönhausen, Lichtenberg, Marzahn, Hellersdorf, Köpenick, Treptow, Neukölln, Tempelhof, Steglitz and Zehlendorf.

Right: *The East Side Gallery makes artistic use of a surviving stretch of the Berlin Wall.*

TOWARDS FRIEDRICHSHAIN

From the front of the Park Inn on Alexanderplatz, the twin carriageway heading to the southeast across the intersection of Gruner Straße and Otto-Braun Straße becomes **Karl-Marx-Allee**, continuing in a straight line towards the inner-city suburb of Friedrichshain. The highway, formerly known as Frankfurter Allee and renamed Stalinallee after World War II, assumed its present identity in 1961 and contains solid 1950s- and 1960s-built apartment blocks, erected to showcase the best Stalinist building traditions. The swanky older buildings, between seven and nine storeys high in tiered *Zuckerbäckerstil* (wedding-cake style), line the section between Strausberger Platz and Frankfurter Tor, their stucco and plaster now peeling.

At **Frankfurter Tor**, a pair of high-rise towers are topped by domes meant to resemble those of the French and German cathedrals on the Gendarmenmarkt. At **Strausberger Platz**, four mighty towers line the way towards the city centre – the route from here in was widened considerably in the early 1960s to double up as a GDR parade ground when required.

East Side Gallery **

When Berlin was divided, the main route south from the centre of East Berlin swept alongside the Wall through some of the dingiest areas of the city. A stretch of

Wall remains, preserved for posterity in all its artistic glory and dubbed the East Side Gallery. The 1.3km (0.8-mile) section is on **Mühlenstraße**, between the **Ostbahnhof** (Eastern Station) and **Warschauer Straße** – on the other side of it flows the Spree. The east-facing side of the open-air gallery originally contained more than 100 contributions by German and foreign artists, done in 1989 to celebrate the reunification of the city. Since 1992 it has been a listed historical monument. The station has changed its name over the years – from Frankfurter Bahnhof to Schlesischer Bahnhof, Ostbahnhof, Hauptbahnhof and back to Ostbahnhof.

Above: *Modern trams at Hackescher Markt – Berlin's tram network survives in the east of the city.*

Volkspark Friedrichshain ★

Berlin's largest park, the Friedrichshain People's Park, was laid out in 1840 to mark the centenary of Friedrich II (Frederick the Great) assuming the throne. While nowhere near the size of the Tiergarten, which it was intended to match, it is crisscrossed by good paths and provides welcome greenery in a heavily urbanized landscape. At its northwestern corner, 1km (0.5 mile) from Alexanderplatz, is the delightful **Märchenbrunnen** (Fairytale Fountain) of 1913, within a semicircular arcade and surrounded by characters taken from tales by the Brothers Grimm. In a cemetery in the southern part of the park are buried nearly 200 demonstrators killed by troops of Friedrich Wilhelm IV during the riots of March 1848; in the northeast corner a monument recalls the joint efforts of the German resistance and Polish soldiers against the Nazis. The two hills in the park are the **Grosse Bunkerberg**, almost 80m (262ft) high, and the smaller **Kleine Bunkerberg**, created by wartime rubble being piled above a pair of bunkers.

DRIVING IN BERLIN

If you are driving to Berlin or hiring a car in the city, you will need a **national driving licence**. Non-Europeans are advised to obtain an **International Driving Permit** in advance. You will also need to carry your vehicle registration documents, a red warning triangle for breakdown emergencies, and a first-aid kit. **Seatbelts** are compulsory for the driver and all passengers. Trams in Berlin automatically have right of way and while they are stationary at designated stops, motorists are not allowed to pass them. The **speed limit** in built-up areas is 50kph (30mph).

Right: *The restored inner courtyards of Hackesche Höfe contain shops, cafés and a film theatre.*

HIRE A BIKE

If walking Berlin's streets on your sightseeing mission starts wearing thin, take to two wheels – hire a bike and pedal off through the **Tiergarten**. There are plenty of cycle lanes in Berlin – often taking up half of the footpath – so you won't have to contend with traffic. The chief bike rental shop in Berlin is **Fahrradstation**, with five branches in the central area. Bikes are carried on the S-Bahn at any time and on the U-Bahn at certain times outside the peak hours.

SCHEUNENVIERTEL

Between Weinmeisterstraße and Rosa-Luxemburg-Platz U-Bahn stations is the Scheunenviertel (Barn Quarter) district. It took its name from the hay barns that were moved here outside the city centre at the end of the 17th century – they were regarded as a potential fire hazard. Before the war, the area was very popular with Jewish immigrant families who arrived in Berlin at nearby Alexanderplatz station. The **Volksbühne Theatre** on Rosa-Luxemburg-Platz, founded by the working class of the district in 1913, had impresario Max Reinhardt as its first director; its reputation for staging provocative productions continues today.

Hackesche Höfe ★★

The eight interconnected **courtyards** near Hackescher Markt, reached through an archway off the southern end of Rosenthaler Straße (Number 40–41), provide a recent and unusual addition to Berlin's attractions. Newly renovated in Art Deco style, they contain shops selling clothes, antiques and books; you can have a picture framed or hire a bike; catch a performance at the film theatre or seek refuge in cafés or restaurants. The first courtyard off Rosenthaler Straße is the finest, with coloured glazed tiles used to create patterns to the top of the five-storey buildings that surround it. Here is the Chamäleon film, music and variety theatre. The buildings date from the turn of the century; their renovation was completed in 1996. Take the S-Bahn to Hackescher Markt, or U-Bahn to Weinmeisterstraße.

ORANIENBURGER STRAßE

Now one of Berlin's most fashionable streets, it links Hackescher Markt with Oranienburger Tor through the middle of the district known as Spandauer Vorstadt (suburb on the way to Spandau). Back in the 1920s the area had something of a Bohemian quality; that spirit is now being recaptured with an influx of bars, ethnic restaurants and centres of culture and art.

In the 1990s, the Scheunenviertel attracted large numbers of squatters, as many buildings were in disrepair. The wrecked building at Number 54–56 with weird artistic appendages adorning its crumbling and graffiti-scribbled façade is the **Galerie Tacheles**, which started life as a Jewish-owned department store in 1909 but was already in financial ruin by the onset of World War I. Permanently under threat of demolition, the Tacheles somehow survives, its flourishing artists co-operative having turned it into a popular venue with studios, a performing area, cinema and café. 'Tacheles', a Yiddish word, roughly translates as 'let's do business'. Heckmann Höfe, at Oranienburger Straße 32, is another series of restored courtyards now housing shops and eateries.

DINING ABOUT

Berlin by night is as fascinating as Berlin by day. Do not restrict your dining out to just one part of the city – clamber aboard a U-Bahn or S-Bahn train and take off to sample the culinary delights of other city areas. In the western city centre, the main restaurant area is centred on the **Ku'damm**, **Kantstraße** and **Savignyplatz** (U-Bahn or S-Bahn to Zoologischer Garten or Savignyplatz), while in Mitte, the **Gendarmenmarkt** and **Friedrichstraße** area (U-Bahn to Französische Straße) offers good dining. Immediately outside the city centre, head for **Oranienburger Straße** (S-Bahn to Hackescher Markt or U-Bahn to Oranienburger Tor); **Prenzlauer Berg** (U-Bahn to Senefelder Platz); or **eastern Kreuzberg** (U-Bahn to Kottbusser Tor).

Below: *Berlin's café life still flourishes.*

KRISTALLNACHT

The night of **9 November 1938**, when the Nazis burnt down 267 synagogues, ransacked 7000 Jewish shops and arrested 26,000 Jews all over Germany, became known as *Kristallnacht* (Night of Broken Glass). It marked a worsening in the **Nazi persecution of the Jews**, with 100 killed and 30,000 sent to concentration camps on that night alone. When the Nazis came to power in 1933, there were 600,000 Jews in Germany; by the end of the war only 12,000 had survived within the country. Today more than 200,000 Jews or people of Jewish descent live in Germany, the figure boosted by immigration from the former Soviet Union.

Neue Synagoge ★★

Berlin's Jewish community, today some 12,000, is centred on Oranienburger Straße and the New Synagogue (**Neue Synagoge**), situated midway along the north side of the street. The synagogue, designed by Eduard Knoblauch, was built between 1859 and 1866 in Moorish-Byzantine style to hold a congregation of 3000. It was Germany's largest synagogue and with its distinctive gilded domes, served as Berlin's chief synagogue until the 1930s. On Kristallnacht (see box, this page), it was saved from being burned down by the action of local police chief Wilhelm Krützfeld, who successfully pleaded with Nazi thugs that the building was a national monument – a plaque on the wall commemorates his brave deed. Though the synagogue was ransacked, it took an Allied bomb in 1943 to finish it off. The synagogue lay in ruins until 1988, when restoration work began; it reopened in May 1995 and is now the **Centrum Judaicum**, recounting Jewish life in the city. A plaque on the building reads 'Vergesst es nie' ('Never forget'). There is a permanent exhibition open Sunday–Monday 10:00–20:00, Tuesday–Thursday 10:00–18:00, Friday 10:00–17:00.

AROUND SOPHIENSTRAßE

The site of Berlin's oldest **Jewish cemetery** (1672) is on the right in Grosse Hamburger Straße, leading off Oranienburger Straße's eastern end. It was destroyed by the

Right: *The New Synagogue on Oranienburger Straße is the hub of Berlin's Jewish community.*

Nazis in 1942. Here, from 1844, stood a Jewish old people's home which the Nazis turned into a detention centre for Berlin's Jewish community before they were dispatched to concentration camps – around 55,000 were sent to their deaths from here and a sculpture of a group of victims now marks the site. Adjacent at Number 27 is the **Jewish school** for boys founded in 1778 by philosopher Moses Mendelssohn (1729–86).

Opposite the school is the **Missing House**, with plaques on the truncated ends of adjacent five-storey buildings recalling those living at Number 11, with their occupations, when it was destroyed in a World War II air raid.

A little further up is the **Sophienkirche** (Sophie's Church), also accessed from Sophienstraße. Named after Princess Sophie Louise, third wife of Friedrich I, it dates from 1712 and is one of Berlin's best Baroque churches. Sophienstraße itself was largely restored in the 1980s and is lined with elegant 19th-century town houses, some containing art and craft workshops. Another set of courtyards, smaller and less visited than the Hackesche Höfe, is found here – the **Sofienhöfe**, with its three courtyards leading through to Gipsstraße.

Above: *The restored Sophienkirche is one of Berlin's best Baroque churches.*

Natural History Museum **

On Invalidenstraße, at Zinnowitzer Straße U-Bahn, is the **Museum für Naturkunde** (Natural History Museum), affiliated to the Humboldt University. It is the largest museum of its kind in Germany and contains a fascinating collection dedicated to the evolution of plants and animals. Highlight is the newly reopened **Dinosaur Hall**, housing the world's largest dinosaur skeleton – the mighty brachiosaurus, 23m (75ft) long and 12m (39ft) high – with half a dozen others well worthy of inspection; here also is a fossilized archaeopteryx bird, showing the connection in evolutionary terms between birds and reptiles. Other exhibits include minerals, meteorites, fossils and coral reefs. Open Tuesday–Friday 09:30–17:00, Saturday–Sunday 10:00–18:00.

PLATFORM FOR ART

The former **Hamburger Bahnhof**, the oldest railway station still standing in Berlin, is home to the **Museum of Contemporary Art**. The museum's centrepieces are the **Erich Marx International Collection** and **Friedrich Christian Flick Collections**, with works by Joseph Beuys, Anselm Kiefer, Robert Rauschenberg, Cy Twombly, Roy Lichtenstein and Andy Warhol. It is situated at Invalidenstraße 50; take the S-Bahn to Hauptbahnhof. Open Tuesday–Friday 10:00–18:00, Saturday 11:00–20:00, Sunday 11:00–18:00.

4
The Western City

While the eastern part of Berlin's city centre has more in the way of historical sights, the western area offers several parks, palaces and the city's leading shopping and nightlife district. It also has **Spreebogen** (the new government area around the new-look Reichstag), as well as museums and the strikingly modern area of **Potsdamer Platz** and **Leipziger Platz**.

REICHSTAG

Just north of the Brandenburg Gate stands the landmark Reichstag (parliament) building, remodelled by British architect **Sir Norman Foster** to house the Lower Chamber of the Bundestag, the Federal German parliament. Developers stripped the building right down to its protected façade in a four-year project, starting in the summer of 1995, that cost £200 million. Surmounted by a **glass dome** above the plenary hall – the original was demolished after World War II and not replaced – the Reichstag's new parliamentary chamber was occupied by the Bundestag for the first time in spring 1999.

The building has endured a chequered history. Designed by **Paul Wallot** in the style of a palace for the parliament of the German Empire, the Renaissance-style building took shape between 1884 and 1894. The tribute *Dem Deutschen Volke* ('To the German People') was added to the Corinthian-columned western front in 1916.

From the Reichstag balcony on 9 November 1918 the German Republic was proclaimed by **Philipp Scheidemann**. And on the night of 27 February 1933 the

DON'T MISS

*** Schloß Charlottenburg: Baroque palace built to rival Versailles.
** Reichstag: newly restored German parliament building.
** Siegessäule: Prussian victory column in the Tiergarten.
** Kulturforum: cultural centre of museums and concert halls.
** Kaiser Wilhelm Memorial Church: instantly familiar war ruin, a symbol of the city.
** Kurfürstendamm: Berlin's world-famous shopping street.

Opposite: *The wooded Tiergarten is situated at the very heart of Berlin.*

Right: *Reichstag visitors queue to tour the glass dome that surmounts the debating chamber in Sir Norman Foster's redesigned parliament building.*
Opposite: *A golden Winged Victory looks down from the top of the Siegessäule column.*

building caught fire – widely held to have been the work of the Nazis, giving them a ready excuse to stamp out parliamentary democracy once and for all and further Hitler's rise to power.

Spreebogen *

New government buildings have risen along the bend in the River Spree immediately north of the Reichstag building, in the northeast corner of the Tiergarten (*see page 63*). Berlin's new parliamentary quarter also includes the **Jakob Kaiser Building**, housing 2000 members of the Bundestag and staff; the **Paul Löbe Building**, which houses the parliamentary committees; and the **Marie-Elisabeth Lüders Building**, housing the library, archives and reference and research services across the Spree River in the former East Berlin. Just north of Spreebogen, a new **Central Station** has been built on the site of the former Lehrter Stadtbahnhof S-Bahn station (*see box, this page*). The new **Tiergarten Tunnel** takes traffic under the park, well away from the new government buildings.

TIERGARTEN

Do not confuse the Tiergarten (Animal Garden) with the adjacent Zoo – Tiergarten is the name given to the extensive wooded area covering 167ha (413 acres) of central Berlin that in the 17th century was a **royal hunting ground**. It was linked to the Royal Castle, the Berliner Schloß, by the avenue that is now Unter den Linden.

NEW RAIL HUB

Berlin has a brand new central railway station on the site of the former suburban **Lehrter Stadtbahnhof**, close to the new Spreebogen government quarter. Designed by Hamburg architect **Meinhard von Gerkan**, Berlin Hauptbahnhof is Europe's most modern and complex mainline station, with lines for long-distance and regional trains, S-Bahn lines and a U-Bahn extension. Construction of the new station was completed in 2006; the entire project cost $850 million.

Siegessäule ★★

In the middle of the Tiergarten at Grosser Stern, traffic swirls around the **Siegessäule** (Victory Column), erected in 1873 by J H Strack to celebrate the Prussian army's victories over Denmark, Austria and France. A gold-plated Winged Victory by Friedrich Drake tops the striking 69m (226ft) high column. The view from the top is superb – but it takes 285 steps to get there. Open Monday–Thursday 09:30–18:30, Friday–Saturday 09:30–19:00 (closes earlier in winter). On the northern edge of Grosser Stern are statues of war leaders Bismarck, Moltke and Roon. At the far end of Straße des 17 Juni, near the Brandenburg Gate, is the **Sowjetisches Ehrenmal** (Soviet War Memorial) of 1946, with the two Russian tanks that led the Russian entry into Berlin in 1945.

Schloß Bellevue ★

From Grosser Stern, Spreeweg heads northeast and on the left is the neoclassical Schloß Bellevue. Prince August Ferdinand, youngest brother of Friedrich II, had the palace built in 1785; it was subsequently used to accommodate guests of the Third Reich and is now the official Berlin residence of the Federal German President. West of the Schloßpark Bellevue is the **Hansaviertel** (the Hansa Quarter), a residential area designed by prominent architects of the time for the 1957 International Building Exposition. The American contribution to the exhibition was a congress hall, renamed **Haus der Kulturen der Welt** (House of World Cultures); it was built in 1957 and is known locally as the 'pregnant oyster'. Nearby the 68-bell **Carillon**, the largest in Europe, chimes daily at midday and 18:00.

> **PARCELLED UP**
>
> Imagine the **Reichstag building** all wrapped up in silver fabric – a preposterous idea indeed. Yet that was what put the long-forgotten Reichstag back into the consciousness of Berliners in 1995 and prepared them for its return to use as the seat of the German parliament. **Bulgarian artist Christo** was commissioned by the Bundestag to cloak the entire building, then without its new Norman Foster-designed dome, in a silver shroud. The spectacle attracted an estimated five million bemused onlookers. Why? they asked. No-one could answer – but they voted the project a total success anyway.

ON A HIGH NOTE

The **Berlin Philharmonic**, one of the world's leading concert orchestras, quickly achieved international recognition after its formation in 1882. Its home is the Philharmonie concert hall at the Kulturforum, known to Berliners as 'Karajan's Circus' because its high, pointed roof is seen as resembling a circus tent. **Herbert von Karajan** led the orchestra until 1989. Its present chief conductor is **Sir Simon Rattle**; previous Berlin Philharmonic directors included **Claudio Abbado**, **Hans von Bülow**, **Artur Nikisch**, **Wilhelm Furtwängler** and **Sergiu Celibidache**.

KULTURFORUM

In the southeastern corner of the Tiergarten, the group of museums and concert venues collectively known as the Kulturforum was largely the work of architect **Hans Scharoun**. Plans for Berlin's new cultural centre took shape in the 1950s and the first building to be completed (in 1963) was the **Philharmonie**, the oddly-shaped gold-coloured concert hall rising behind the trees only a short distance away from the grand high-rises of Potsdamer Platz. It is now the home of the world-famous Berlin Philharmonic Orchestra.

There is a direct link from the Philharmonie to the **Musikinstrumenten Museum** (Musical Instruments Museum) of 1985, with its excellent collection of string, wind and keyboard instruments from the 16th century – everything can be found here, from ancient harpsichords to modern synthesizers and even a 1929 Wurlitzer cinema organ. Open Tuesday–Friday 09:00–17:00 (Thursday to 22:00), Saturday–Sunday 10:00–17:00. On the opposite side of the Philharmonie is the much smaller **Kammermusiksaal** (Chamber Music Hall) from 1987.

Art appreciation comes in rather large doses at the Kulturforum, with no fewer than three important venues. The newest is the **Gemäldegalerie** (New Picture Gallery), which opened in June 1998 and houses a major collection of works from the 13th to the 18th centuries, from Van Eyck to Tizian, Raffael to Caravaggio, Rembrandt to Rubens. There are Italian paintings from the 14th to the 18th centuries, Dutch works of the 15th and 16th centuries and German paintings from the late Gothic and Renaissance periods. It's open daily (except Monday) from 10:00–18:00 (Thursday to 22:00). Around 900 paintings hang in the main gallery and more than 400 in the studio gallery. The collection was founded by the Great Elector, Friedrich Wilhelm, in the mid-17th century, extended by Friedrich II (Frederick the Great) 100 years later, and continued by Wilhelm von Bode until his death in 1929.

The **Kunstgewerbe-museum** (the Decorative Arts Museum) close by displays arts and crafts from medieval times right up to the present day; it includes gold work from the Middle Ages and the Renaissance, the 12th-century Welfenschatz (the Welf treasure), the Lüneburger Ratssilber (the Lüneburg silver collection), and furniture of the 16th to the 18th centuries, as well as textile art. The **Kupferstichkabinett** (Museum of Prints and Drawings) contains an important collection of drawings and prints from the Middle Ages onwards, highlights of which include contributions by Albrecht Dürer, Pieter Breughel the Elder and Rembrandt. Opening times for both are Tuesday–Friday 10:00–18:00, Saturday–Sunday 11:00–18:00.

The **Neue Nationalgalerie**, to the south fronting Potsdamerstraße, was built from 1965–68 on a partly underground plinth to a design by **Ludwig Mies van der Rohe** – the paintings are displayed on the underground floor of the gallery, with exhibitions staged upstairs. It contains 20th-century German expressionist works by Kirchner and Schmidt-Rottluf, Bauhaus works (Feiniger, Klee, Schlemmer), New Objectivity (Dix, Grosz) and Post-War (Ernst, Picasso). Across Potsdamerstraße is Scharoun's massive **Staatsbibliothek** (National Library), which opened in 1978 and houses more than 10 million volumes.

Above: *The gold-coloured Philharmonie sits at the heart of the Kulturforum.*

CUTTING THE COST

Berlin's best offer for visitors is the **WelcomeCard**, offering two or three days' travel within the city and Potsdam and discounts from 25 per cent on a range of attractions. It is well suited to **families**, as the holder can be accompanied by up to three children under the age of 14. The card can be bought at the offices of BVG (the public transport network), at tourist information points, S-Bahn, DB Regio, in many of Berlin's hotels and online.

Above: *Kaiser Wilhelm Memorial Church seen through a large sculpture on Tauentzienstraße.*

AROUND THE ZOO

The lively and colourful hub of Berlin's western centre stretches between the Zoologischer Garten railway station and the Europa-Center. To the south of the station, the Kurfürstendamm shopping and nightlife avenue leads off westwards; on Breitscheidplatz itself stands another famous symbol of Berlin, the ruined Kaiser Wilhelm Memorial Church; and to the east, opposite the zoo entrance, are the indoor Europa-Center shopping complex and KaDeWe, Europe's largest department store.

Kaiser Wilhelm Memorial Church ★★

The **Kaiser-Wilhelm-Gedächtniskirche** (Kaiser Wilhelm Memorial Church), with its bomb-shattered tower and spire, is an instantly recognizable symbol of Berlin. The neo-Romanesque church was built in 1895 as a memorial to Kaiser Wilhelm I, but fell victim to Allied bombing on 22 November 1943, which left just the severely damaged western end standing. The remains stand as a memorial both to the horrors of World War II and the devastation suffered by Berlin. Alongside the ruins, the modern octagonal church and hexagonal bell tower, added in 1959–61 with their rich blue French stained glass from Chartres, symbolize the postwar rebirth of Berlin – they quickly earned the Berliners' sobriquet 'lipstick' and 'make-up box'. A small **museum** contains pictures of before and after the bombing. The museum is open daily 09:00–19:00; the ruined tower and exhibitions are open Monday–Saturday 10:00–16:00.

Kurfürstendamm ★★

Originally a riding track connecting the Tiergarten with the Grunewald forest to the southwest, it was surfaced in the 1880s and is now Berlin's prime **shopping** street, lined with department stores, fashion houses and boutiques. Theatres,

---

KIDS' DELIGHT

City breaks can be fun for the children, too. Take them to the **Zoo** at the Tiergarten and introduce them to its star, the giant panda Bao Bao, or the **Tierpark Berlin** in Lichtenberg, the city's second zoo. Fascinate them in the **Märkisches Museum**, where they will enjoy the noisy display of 18th-century mechanical instruments called automatones. Pressing buttons at the **Deutsches Technikmuseum** will amuse them for hours, as will the museum's Spectrum building, designed for experimentation. In the **Museum für Naturkunde** they will wonder at the scale of the dinosaurs on display.

cinemas, restaurants, bars and cafés fill the spaces between the shops, along with the multimedia **Berlin Story** attraction at 207–8, complete with radiation-proof bunker. A worthwhile stopping point is the **Café Kranzler** next to Ku'damm U-Bahn station. The café, founded in 1835, was resited after the war from its original location on the corner of Friedrichstraße and Unter den Linden.

Europa-Center ★

The modern building at the eastern end of Breitscheidplatz beneath the revolving Mercedes star houses the multi-tiered shopping emporium of the Europa-Center, with its Flow of Time Clock (*see* box, this page) and pleasant interior water garden. Outside the Europa-Center, the pink granite **Weltbrunnen** (Fountain of the World) from 1983 is a popular resting place for bagladen tourists staggering from **KaDeWe** (an abbreviation of *Kaufhaus des Westens*, the Department Store of the West), which claims to be Europe's largest.

KaDeWe looks out on to Wittenbergplatz, with its neoclassical U-Bahn station and memorial to concentration camp victims. The list of 12 camps within a steel frame is a simple commemoration of the Nazi atrocities; it exhorts the German people 'never to forget'.

KEEPING TIME

Berlin has a penchant for unusual clocks. As well as the **Weltzeituhr** (World Time Clock) on Alexanderplatz, there are two very different timepieces at the Europa-Center. Inside the centre, shoppers stand mesmerized by the fluorescent green liquid coursing through the glass veins and spheres of Bernard Gitton's **Flow of Time Clock**. Outside the centre, visitors attempt to make sense of the cluster of red and yellow lights of the **Mengenlehre** (set theory) **Clock**. Lights on the top row represent five hours, the second row one hour, third row five minutes and fourth row one minute. Erected on the Ku'damm in June 1975, it was moved to its present site at the tourist office entrance in 1996.

Below: *The gently cascading Fountain of the World is situated next to the Europa-Center.*

BRISTOL FASHION

The name Hotel Bristol, echoing days when Bristol was the UK's chief embarkation port for transatlantic liners, is found in cities throughout the world. In Berlin, the **Hotel Bristol Kempinski** on the Ku'damm was the first hotel to be built after World War II, opening in 1952 on the site of the original Kempinski deli-catessen and restaurant, which opened in 1926. Berliners know the hotel as the 'Kempi'; step inside to inspect its impressive spiral staircase, regarded as a city treasure.

Below: *A sculpture of the prominent Berlin artist Käthe Kollwitz in Prenzlauer Berg.*

The Zoo ★★

With around 14,000 animals embracing 1500 species, Berlin's zoo is the oldest in Germany – it opened in 1844 on Tiergarten land donated by Friedrich Wilhelm IV – and one of the largest in the world. It occupies the southwest corner of the Tiergarten, extending as far as the Landwehrkanal, and is reached through the splendid **Elephant Gate** entrance opposite the Europa-Center on Budapester Straße. The adjacent aquarium opened in 1869. Open daily 09:00–18:00/dusk.

Kantstraße ★

The **Erotik Museum**, with its surprisingly tasteful array of exhibits on the corner of Joachimstaler Straße, makes a striking contrast to the **Karstadt** store opposite, where four floors are packed with sports gear and equipment. Beyond the railway bridge, the cluster of entertainment venues is fronted by the **Theater des Westens**, created by Bernard Sehring in 1896. After serving postwar as Berlin's opera house, the theatre is now one of the top European stages for musical productions. Behind it are the **Delphi Film Palace**, popular **Quasimodo** jazz and blues nightspot and **Vaganten Bühne** theatre.

Käthe-Kollwitz-Museum ★★

A collection of sculptures, drawings, prints and posters by Berlin's greatest female artist Käthe Kollwitz (*see* box, opposite page), many focusing on war and poverty, fills the restored 1870s villa at Fasanenstraße 24. The house, partly destroyed in World War II, was acquired for the museum in 1984. Open daily 11:00–18:00, closed Tuesday; taped audio tours available.

At Fasanenstraße 79–80, beyond the Ku'damm, the **Jüdisches Gemeindehaus** (Jewish Community House) embraces part of a synagogue destroyed by the Nazis on *Kristallnacht* (9 November 1938), as well as a highly rated kosher restaurant.

Left: *The imposing Elephant Gate entrance to Berlin Zoo.*

Beyond Savignyplatz ★

Kantstraße bisects leafy **Savignyplatz**, named after the Prussian Minister of Justice, Friedrich Karl von Savigny. Beyond the suburban shopping street of **Wilmersdorfer Straße**, Kantstraße leads to the **Messegelände** (Exhibition Grounds), with its circle of exhibition halls built on Hitler's orders. In their midst stands the **Funkturm** (radio tower) from the late 1920s; from its viewing platform nearly 130m (427ft) you can look down on a section of Autobahn laid out as Germany's first motor-racing track in the 1920s and the futuristic silver-grey **ICC** (International Congress Centre) building from the 1970s.

An overview of Berlin can be obtained from a viewing gallery 55m (180ft) up the **Grunewaldturm** (Grunewald Tower), a memorial to Kaiser Wilhelm I in the Grunewald, 4km (2.5 miles) south of the Exhibition Grounds. Next to Grunewaldsee is the **Jagdschloß Grunewald**, dating from 1542–43 and now housing an art collection.

Olympic Stadium ★

The showpiece built by **Werner March** for Hitler's staging of the 1936 Olympic Games, 8km (5 miles) west of the city centre, was given a costly facelift for the 2006 finals of the World Cup football tournament staged in Germany. Here, American runner Jesse Owens won four gold medals, soundly disputing the Nazi claim of Aryan supremacy. Bundesliga soccer club Hertha Berlin now uses the 75,000-seat stadium.

KÄTHE KOLLWITZ

Berlin's greatest woman artist was born on 8 July 1867 in Königsberg (now Kaliningrad) and from 1891 lived for almost 50 years in Weissenburger Straße (now called Kollwitzstraße) in the city's **Prenzlauer Berg** district. War, poverty, motherhood and death were oft-recurring themes in her work and she displayed enormous versatility in her sculptures, drawings, lithographs and woodcuts. Her **drawings** included many self-portraits; **woodcuts** include the series of seven from 1922–23 entitled *Krieg* (War) and two entitled *Proletariat* of 1925. The bronze *Mutter mit Zwillingen* (Mother with Twins), dating from 1927–37, is one of her best-known **sculptures**.

Above: *The Schloß Charlottenburg was to rival Versailles.*
Opposite: *The palace gardens show a mix of styles.*

PRICEY PALACE

Leading fashion designer **Karl Lagerfeld** was responsible for the interior decor of Berlin's highest-priced hotel, the **Schloßhotel Im Grunewald**, now a listed historical monument. The hotel started life as the **Palais Pannwitz**, completed in Baroque style in 1914 for Dr Walther von Pannwitz; the first guest at the house was **Kaiser Wilhelm II**, a friend of the family. Lagerfeld took on the artistic direction when it was converted to a private luxury hotel and keeps his own apartment there. Since it opened in 1994, the 52-room hotel, at Brahmsstraße 10 in Grunewald, has hosted visiting royalty and many top foreign politicians.

SCHLOß CHARLOTTENBURG

Initially intended as a summer retreat for Sophie Charlotte, the wife of the future King Friedrich I, the modest dwelling designed by **Arnold Nering** in 1695 was considerably enlarged over the next 100 years to reflect the growing power of the ruling Hohenzollerns. Architects of the Baroque palace included Johann Friedrich Eosander, Georg von Knobelsdorff and Carl Gotthard Langhans.

Even before Sophie Charlotte died in 1705 at the age of 37, Friedrich I had commissioned Eosander to develop the building along the lines of Versailles. At its centre is the **Nering-Eosander Building**, housing the quarters of the Hohenzollerns; also the **Porcelain Room**, stacked to the ceiling with Chinese and Japanese figurines and tableware, and the **Chapel**. The dome was a 1712 addition by Eosander, complete with the goddess Fortuna atop.

The east **Knobelsdorff Wing** is a reconstruction of the architect's 1746 original design, containing ceremonial upstairs rooms such as the pristine **White Hall**, which was formerly the dining room, and the gilded **Golden Gallery**. Adjacent is the **Concert Room**. All feature 18th-century works of French masters such as Watteau, Pesne and Boucher. The ground-level **Romantics Gallery** contains outstanding works by 19th-century Romantics such as Caspar David Friedrich and Carl Blechen, along with examples of Classical, Biedermeier and Nazarene art.

The west wing, known as the **Langhans Building**, houses the **Museum of Pre- and Early History**, with archaeological finds. The second-floor collection of Trojan antiquities assembled by Heinrich Schliemann (1822–90), the discoverer of Troy, is the museum's highlight. Severely bombed in 1943, the palace was rebuilt in the original style between 1950 and 1965.

The Gardens ★

The gardens of Schloß Charlottenburg are a mix of formal French and manicured English styles. They contain the Italian-style **Schinkel Pavilion**, built by Karl Friedrich Schinkel in 1824 for the summer use of Friedrich Wilhelm III – it contains drawings by the architect, as well as paintings and sculptures. The neoclassical **Mausoleum**, on the west side of the park, contains the tombs of Friedrich Wilhelm III (1770–1840), his wife Queen Luise (1776–1810) and Kaiser Wilhelm I. On the opposite side of the lake is the **Belvedere**, built by Langhans in 1788 as a teahouse for Friedrich Wilhelm II and now housing a collection of royal Berlin porcelain. Open Tuesday–Friday 09:00–17:00, Saturday–Sunday 10:00–17:00.

The Other Museums ★★

South of Spandauer Damm on Schloßstraße is the **Museum Berggruen**, its classic modern art collection including works by Picasso, Klee, Giacometti and Matisse. The collection in the West Stühler Building focuses on Picasso, with more than 100 works, including his blue and pink period. The museum is open daily (except Monday) from 10:00–18:00. Here, too, is the **Bröhan-Museum**, dedicated to the decorative arts, from Art Nouveau to Functionalism, with paintings, sculptures, graphics, arts and crafts. The **Heimatmuseum Charlottenburg** is the local history museum.

SOCCER IN BERLIN

Soccer is king in Germany (the West Germans won the **World Cup** on three occasions) and **Hertha Berlin** is the capital's leading club. In GDR days, **Dynamo Berlin** ruled the roost on the eastern side of the Wall, winning their own national championship no fewer than 10 times. After a spell as FC Berlin, the club restored 'Dynamo' to its title and now plays in a lower league as Berliner FC Dynamo. The **Bundesliga** cup finals held at the Olympic Stadium pull in crowds of 75,000 each year.

5
The New Heart

Nowhere in a divided Berlin was the tragedy of the Wall more evident than on **Potsdamer Platz** – Europe's busiest square before the war – and **Leipziger Platz**. When the Wall went up in 1961, the concrete ribbon cut through a part of the city that, decades earlier, had epitomized the very soul of Berlin. Street signs in the West pointed vaguely across the death strip; truncated tram lines led nowhere; it was impossible to imagine the streets packed with buildings and shops that, badly bombed in the war, had become lost in the infamous no-man's-land between the two parts of a divided city.

Until the end of 1989, it was an area of derelict waste ground, watched over by armed GDR border guards. Tourist buses would unload their passengers here so that they could climb up to viewing platforms and peer over the Wall, across the strip and into the dismal, depressing communist world beyond that most did not care to visit. A handful of snack bars and souvenir kiosks did good business, but otherwise there was no commercial activity of any kind on the edge of this urban wasteland.

What a difference now! Emerge into the daylight at Potsdamer Platz U-Bahn station today and before you is Berlin's shining new 'city within a city', a high-rise development of gleaming glass and steel filling the 49ha (120 acres) between Potsdamer Platz and Leipziger Platz. It is the end product of Europe's biggest ever **construction project** that had been taking shape in planners' minds since the day the border opened. Long before its completion, Berlin had again become a seamless city.

BERLIN

DON'T MISS

** Haus am Checkpoint Charlie: museum tracing the history of the Wall.
** Berlin Wall: just a small fragment remains of this Cold War relic.
** Deutsches Technikmuseum: for a hands-on approach to technology.
** Jüdisches Museum: chronicles the life of Berlin's Jewish population.
** New Potsdamer Platz: shopping and entertainment heart of the new Berlin.

Opposite: *An eye-catching piece of contemporary artwork in the Potsdamer Platz development.*

20

OPEN ON MONDAYS

Many Berlin attractions take Monday off, but not all. Museums and exhibitions open for business on Mondays include the **Centrum Judaicum**, the **Erotik Museum**, **Haus am Checkpoint Charlie**, **Käthe-Kollwitz-Museum** and the **Puppentheater-Museum** in Karl-Marx-Straße, Neukölln (open 09:30–17:00). On Mondays you can also visit Berlin's two **zoos** (the Zoo-logischer Garten and Tierpark Berlin), the **Berliner Dom**, **Staatsbibliothek** and **Haus der Wannsee Konferenz**.

POTSDAMER PLATZ

The meeting point of five busy Berlin roads, Potsdamer Platz was named in 1831 after the nearby Potsdamer Tor (Potsdam Gate), built by **Schinkel** seven years earlier as a southern entrance to the city. By the 1920s, up to 100,000 people a day were pouring into the square, jostling for space with 20,000 cars and a huge fleet of trams.

With World War II came the end of an era for Potsdamer Platz. Around 80 per cent of buildings on the square were destroyed by Allied bombing, and the blitzed and battered area never recovered. After the war the square found itself at the confluence of the British, American and Russian-controlled sectors of the city and became the centre of a major **black market**. But by 1961 any contact between the occupying powers was lost when the **Wall** that bisected the city was built right here, turning the area into a destitute wasteland for the ensuing 28 years – a scar on the city landscape that symbolized the division of Germany. Traffic once again began to flow across the former 'death strip' on 12 November 1989, three days after the opening of the Wall.

The Berlin Wall ★

The bits of Wall that survive on the corner of Ebertstraße and Potsdamer Platz are but a fragment of the original 165km (103-mile) barrier that ring-fenced West Berlin, the part of the city under British, American and French control. Its construction followed East Germany's closure of the border with West Berlin on 13 August 1961, on the orders of Soviet leader **Nikita Khrushchev**, to halt emigration to the west. Since the GDR's formation in 1949, three million East Germans had fled to the

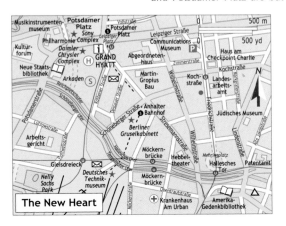

The New Heart

Federal Republic seeking a better life in the West, half of them through Berlin. While the barbed wire barricades stemmed the flow of refugees, a few still managed to escape across the border – many died in the attempt, among the first of around 190 lives lost in courageous attempts to flee to the West.

On 15 August, the building of the Wall (*Die Mauer*) began – in the eyes of the GDR authorities it was a permanent solution to a problem that was already out of hand, depriving the communist state of more and more of its skilled workers. The Wall, complete with its 'death strip' of **watchtowers** populated by binocular-wielding border guards under shoot-to-kill orders, followed the Soviet sector boundary north-south across the city, bisecting streets and squares, crossing rivers and causing the demolition of anything in its way.

Though crossing points were quickly established for foreigners, regulations allowing 'Wessies' to visit the East were not drawn up until as late as 1971. The main crossing point was **Checkpoint Charlie** on Friedrichstraße (*see* page 81).

New Potsdamer Platz ★
Berlin's challenge to become the unofficial capital of Europe took root at New Potsdamer Place on 11 October 1993 with ground-breaking at the start of a **building project** on a scale larger than even London's Docklands. The £1.3 billion development bridging the gap between the former western and eastern city centres, funded by the A+T group, Sony Corporation and Daimler-Benz (now Daimler Chrysler) is immense and offers the visitor an ultra-modern aspect of the city in strong contrast to all that's around.

Above: *Colourful artwork and information on a fragment of the Belin Wall at Potsdamer Platz.*

PIECES OF HATE

Rough fragments of Berlin's 165km (103-mile) **Wall**, complete with snatches of graffiti, are now scattered throughout the world, the souvenir remnants of a failed political system. The Berlin Wall was built from a pale-coloured aggregate of flint, pebbles and other hard material. It stood 4m (13ft) high, the tubular top added in a bid to foil escape attempts. On the GDR side, manned **watchtowers** with searchlights overlooked a sandy **no-man's-land** up to 150m (164yd) wide that contained **tripwires** and patrolling **dogs**. East German **border guards** were ordered to shoot on sight anyone trying to escape.

Above: *The steel and glass Sony Plaza is a key part of the Potsdamer Platz development.*

BUILDING BOOM

Berlin's massive **redevelopment** is on a scale never before seen in Europe. Some €150 billion (£103 billion) was invested in reshaping the city's heart up to 2005. Six million tonnes of excavated earth and 200,000 tonnes of rubble and debris were carted away from the big city-centre sites in **Tiergarten** and **Mitte**, while about 17 million tonnes of building materials were required – enough to fill a train stretching from Berlin to Rome and back.

For an overview of the complex take Europe's fastest elevator (it whisks you up 23 floors in just 20 seconds) to the top of the Thyssenkrupp building on the Daimler Chrysler complex – it's the highest building in the new heart of Berlin, designed by the Berlin architect Hans Kollhoff. From here you can see key landmarks like the Brandenburg Gate, Reichstag and Berliner Dom.

An international team of architects created the **Daimler Chrysler complex**, with 19 buildings that took just four years to erect. They include the towering Daimler Chrysler building with its atrium sculptures; the triple-tier, glass-roofed **Arkaden** indoor shopping mall with its 110 retail outlets and avenue of trees; more than 30 restaurants, cafés and bars; and an **entertainment complex** on Marlene-Dietrich-Platz featuring the Theater by Potsdamer Platz, Blue Max Theater, 3500-seat Cinemaxx movie complex, Adagio nightspot and casino. There is also a luxury hotel, the 340-room **Grand Hyatt Berlin**, more than 600 residential apartments and many offices. Fountains and other water attractions provide some relief among the buildings.

Across Neue Potsdamer Straße, the steel and glass **Sony Plaza** contains the company's European headquarters and was opened in June 2000. The Filmmuseum Berlin, with its Marlene Dietrich artefacts and a multiplex cinema, occupy the building; outside is a Legoland park. The third complex here is the **A+T Park Colonnades**. A short way east of Potsdamer Platz, work on the **Leipziger Platz** development continued simultaneously and the whole area now presents a very different face of Berlin to the world.

The whole development, southwest of the original Potsdamer Platz site, is served by the U-Bahn and S-Bahn stations at Potsdamer Platz and a new station, Mendelssohn-Bartholdy Park, on U-Bahn line U2. There are 4000 car parking spaces on site.

ROAD SIGNS

Autobahn • Motorway
Bleifrei • Lead-free
Durchgang verboten •
No thoroughfare
Einbahnstraße •
One-way street
Eingang/Ausgang •
Entrance/exit
Nur Fussgänger •
Pedestrians only
Parkplatz • Parking place
Strassenbahnhalt • Tram stop
Umleitung • Diversion
Vorsicht • Take care

AROUND ANHALTER BAHNHOF

On Askanischer Platz, to the east of the swanky new Potsdamer Platz high-rises, the ruined entrance arches of what was once Berlin's grandest railway station stand forlornly alone above an underground stretch of the S-Bahn. The station, built in 1840, served as Berlin's southern gateway, from where trains departed for Anhalt, Munich and Dresden.

A little way up Stresemannstraße, the Third Reich headquarters of the Gestapo, SS and Nazi security service once stood. An **exhibition** on the site, the *Topographie des Terrors* (the Topography of Terror), documents the crimes commited in the Nazi era. The exhibition is open daily 10:00–20:00 (October–April 10:00–18:00). On nearby Niederkirchner Straße is the **Martin Gropius building**, which was constructed in

Below: *This is all that is left of Anhalter Bahnhof terminus, once one of Berlin's busiest railway stations.*

COFFEE BREAK

Berliners like to take their coffee strong and preferably unfiltered – the **Turkish** way that you will find offered in countless bars and cafés around **Kreuzberg** in particular. At the turn of the century there were many small and inexpensive coffee houses around the city, called *Kaffeeklappen*. Around **Unter den Linden** and **Friedrichstraße** at that time there were also **Viennese**-style cafés with news-papers for patrons to read – a tradition that is still followed by Berlin café owners. Today, city-centre cafés dispense all kinds of coffee – espresso, regular, cappuccino or whatever takes your fancy.

Opposite: *A tourist poses for a souvenir photo at Checkpoint Charlie.*
Below: *Coffee is served all over town – even at the TV Tower.*

ornate Renaissance style between 1877 and 1881 as the Museum of Applied Arts by Martin Gropius, the great uncle of Bauhaus architect Walter Gropius, and Heino Schmieden. After severe wartime damage, it was restored in 1981 and is today Berlin's most important exhibition hall.

Moving down Schöneberger Straße, the **Berliner Gruselkabinett** is the only wartime air-raid shelter open to the public. Its three floors contain widely varying exhibits and effects – there is a chamber of horrors on the upper floor, a display of gruesome medieval surgery on the ground floor and, in the basement, an exhibition showing the wartime role of the building, with its 2m (6.5ft) thick walls.

Deutsches Technikmuseum ★★

Spread over several buildings on the site of the former **Anhalter railway depot** at Trebbiner Straße 9, the Deutsches Technikmuseum (the German Museum of Technology) approaches a complex subject in a simple and practical way, covering the field with hands-on exhibits, demonstrations and experiments. A compre-hensive transportation section covers railways, cars, shipping and aircraft; other areas feature industrial, infor-mation, energy and printing technologies; film and photography; scientific instruments and plenty more. The **Science Center Spectrum** at Möckernstraße 26 allows visitors to con-firm many basic technological princi-ples by undertaking more than 200 experi-ments on their own. It is open Tuesday–Friday from 09:00–17:30, Saturday–Sunday 10:00–18:00.

AROUND CHECKPOINT CHARLIE

Travelling the small distance from West Berlin into East Berlin during the time before the Wall came down was rather an involved procedure. Foreigners were required to negotiate the border crossing that was known as Checkpoint Charlie – so-called because it was the third Allied checkpoint, known by its phonetic name (C for Charlie). As a pedestrian on a day visit, you shuffled from one dowdy prefabricated building to another while East German officials treble-checked your pass-

port, made copious notes and eventually issued the piece of paper that allowed you in until midnight – on payment of 25 Marks, for which you received 25 non-refundable Ostmarks. As a motorist, you were subjected to the most thorough vehicle search before the green barrier was raised.

Now Checkpoint Charlie is really little more than a memory. Almost nothing at all remains of the once infamous demarcation line between the American and Russian sectors of Berlin, where tanks of the two armies stood facing each other in October 1961 in a particularly unsavoury incident of the Cold War. In the middle of Friedrichstraße, suspended portraits of American and Soviet soldiers mark the line of the east-west border and tourists pose for pictures with uniformed personnel. The sign that lets you know 'You are now leaving the American sector' is a copy. A section of the Wall exists to the west of Checkpoint Charlie, along Zimmerstraße past the intersection with Wilhelmstraße.

NOW READ ON ...

Though no English-language **newspapers** are published in Berlin, you can keep abreast of world affairs with the widely circulated *International Herald Tribune*. Most English newspapers are on sale, as is *USA Today*. National papers published in Berlin include *Die Welt*; there are also several Berlin publications, including *Berliner Morgenpost*, *Berliner Zeitung* and *Der Tagesspiegel*. Berlin has an amazing array of **radio** stations; for a worldwide update, tune in to the BBC World Service on 90.2FM. There is English-language **TV** output on Deutsche Welle, CNN and BBC World.

Haus am Checkpoint Charlie ★★★

The chief point of interest in the vicinity of the old checkpoint is the Haus am Checkpoint Charlie, on the corner of Friedrichstraße and Kochstraße, a privately run, fascinating and usually crowded **museum** that tells the history of the Wall and chronicles the many escape attempts made since its erection in 1961. What started out as a small group of exhibits in a couple of rooms on the street corner now extends above several shop fronts along Friedrichstraße and contains photos, graphic accounts of escape attempts and some of the equipment used by refugees – from a hot-air balloon to skilfully adapted vehicles and specially constructed suitcases. Two films show in the cinema – 'Mit dem Wind nach Westen', a balloon flight to the west, and 'Mein Kampf', a documentary about the Third Reich. There are also showings of **documentary films** throughout the day on the division of Germany and the wider struggle for human rights. The museum is open daily 09:00–22:00.

Jüdisches Museum ★★

The striking vision of Polish-born American architect **Daniel Libeskind** was responsible for the dramatic angled design of the building on Lindenstraße – named after him – that houses the Jüdisches Museum (Jewish Museum). The Jewish Museum was opened in 2001, including the **art** and **history** collection previously on display in the Martin-Gropius-Bau that vividly portrayed the life of Berlin's Jewish population, the largest Jewish community in Germany in pre-Nazi times. There were about 60,000 Jewish people living in Berlin at the outbreak of World War II, of whom 50,000 died in concentration camps. The collection has been extended to provide a comprehensive

---

FREE IN BERLIN

You do not always have to dig deep to finance your stay in Berlin. Many museums do not charge admission on the first Sunday of the month, and for other museums and exhibitions there is free admission at all times. They include:

• the **Allierten Museum** at Clayallee 135, Zehlendorf, covering the Allied powers' stay in Berlin from 1945–94;

• the **'Path to Parliamentary Democracy in Germany'** historical exhibition in the German Cathedral on Gendarmenmarkt;

• the **Museum Berlin-Karlshorst** at Zwieseler Straße 4 in Lichtenberg, site of Germany's World War II surrender.

• **Haus der Wannsee Konferenz** at Am Grossen Wannsee 56 in Zehlendorf, housing an exhibition on the Wannsee Conference and extermination of European Jews.

picture of German-Jewish history, rather than just Berlin's Jewish population. A branch of the Leo Baeck Institute in New York has been open at the Jüdische Museum since 2001. The entrance is through the former Collegienhaus, a Baroque courthouse from the 1730s and western Berlin's oldest building. The two-storey, three-winged building was due to have a Libeskind-designed glass roof installed above its courtyard in 2007. The museum is open daily 10:00–20:00 (Mondays 10:00–22:00).

Amerika-Gedenkbibliothek ★

The southern end of Friedrichstraße, a few blocks from the Checkpoint Charlie site, brings you to the wide, circular **Mehringplatz** – two semicircular high-rises with a column at their centre commemorating the Prussian army's victory over Napoleon's forces in 1815. This is the mid-point of the **Landwehrkanal**, the narrow 19th-century waterway that cuts a route south of the city centre, joining the Lower Spree west of the Tiergarten and Upper Spree north of Treptow. Barges laden with all manner of goods once used the canal; now only pleasure boats ply up and down. Across the canal on Blücher-platz is the **Amerika-Gedenkbibliothek** (the America Memorial Library), built to mark the Berlin Airlift of 1948–49 and said to contain some 800,000 items.

BERLIN'S ORACLE

Berlin has the world's first street oracle in **Mehringplatz**, at the southern end of Friedrichstraße. It takes the form of 64 coloured **metal panel flags** arranged in a circle on the roof of a tower in the same order as that of the spectrum – they are the sign of the oracle. Approach the oracle and ask yourself a question that you cannot answer with a simple 'yes' or 'no'. Move to the colour you like best and read the oracle's answer at the foot of the panel, inspired by the 2500-year-old Chinese Book of Changes, I Ching.

Opposite: A Trabant car painted by Thierry Noir outside Haus am Checkpoint Charlie, the museum dedicated to the Berlin Wall.
Left: The Café Adler, a former pharmacy on Friedrichstraße, was the last building in West Berlin before the Checkpoint Charlie border crossing.

6
The Inner Suburbs

After the stone and steel sterility of Potsdamer Platz, two rather more fascinating inner-city districts are welcomingly but a few U-Bahn stops away – **Kreuzberg** in the southeast and **Prenzlauer Berg** to the northeast. Each of these areas has evolved from its distinctly working-class background to become a focus of the 'Alternative Berlin' scene, with a strong emphasis on the **arts** and **nightlife**.

KREUZBERG

Home to the largest community of **Turkish** people outside Turkey itself, Kreuzberg has evolved as a district of two very distinct halves – western Kreuzberg, which lies to the south of the former Checkpoint Charlie (*see* page 81), and eastern Kreuzberg, where the atmosphere is as much Middle Eastern as it is central European.

For a period of almost 30 years, Kreuzberg lived in the shadow of the Berlin Wall, an overlooked backwater of the western city where a great many of its approximately 150,000 inhabitants lived in crumbling and overcrowded **tenement buildings**. Squatting was commonplace then, and the authorities appeared to turn a blind eye. But though the tenements, many of which were built in the early 1900s, are still there, Kreuzberg is no longer the dropout domain of students, hippies and artists it once was. The increase in property values since reunification has refined the area's image and it is becoming an increasingly sought-after part of the city in which to live and work.

DON'T MISS

** **Eastern Kreuzberg:** for inner-city Turkish atmosphere.
** **Prenzlauer Berg:** newly fashionable dining and drinking district.
* **Rathaus Schöneberg:** former city hall where US president JF Kennedy spoke.
* **Tierpark Berlin:** among the largest zoos in Europe.

Opposite: *With its colourful street art and Middle Eastern atmosphere, Kreuzberg is very much part of the 'Alternative Berlin' scene.*

TURKISH DELIGHTS

If a visit to Kreuzberg's Turkish quarter whets your appetite for **Turkish cuisine**, try one of the Berlin restaurants specializing in this type of fare:

• **Iskele**, at Planufer 83, Kreuzberg, Berlin's oldest restaurant boat;

• **Miro**, at Raumerstraße 29, Prenzlauer Berg, is a relatively expensive venue;

• **Terra Anatolia**, at Hauptstraße 65, Schöneberg, where specialities include dishes baked in a special Anatolian oven;

• **Hitit**, at Knobelsdorffstraße 35, Charlottenburg, has a splendid marble fountain in its midst.

Western Kreuzberg ★

The district of Kreuzberg is named after the hill in its southwest corner, most of which is covered by the **Viktoriapark**, laid out in the first part of the 19th century by Gustav Meyer. The elegant 20m (66ft) **steeple** at the park's highest point, 66m (217ft) up, is a memorial to the 1815 Napoleonic war by Karl Friedrich Schinkel that takes the form of a cross (*Kreuz* in German). There are streams, ponds and a man-made waterfall in the park, the southern side of which slopes down to the Schultheiss brewery.

Just north of the park is one of those attractions to be found only in Berlin – the **Schwules Museum** (Gay Museum), on the third floor in the second courtyard at Mehringdamm 61. Open daily (except Tuesday) 14:00–18:00 (Saturday to 19:00). To the west of Mehringdamm's intersection with Yorckstraße is the twin-spired, neo-Gothic **St Bonifatius-Kirche**; around the corner in Grossbeerenstraße you come upon the **Riehmers Hofgarten**, a residential complex built for Berlin's better-off citizens at the turn of the century. Among the many local fringe theatres and theatre workshops are the **Mehringhof-Theater**, staging contemporary and political

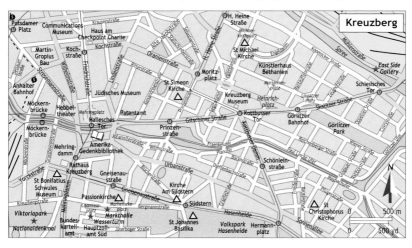

cabaret near the Mehring-Yorck intersection, and a couple of streets east, on Schwiebusserstraße, the **Zerbrochene Fenster** (Broken Window).

East of Viktoriapark, Bergmannstraße with its cafés and second-hand bookshops bisects western Kreuzberg on its way to the spacious **Volkspark Hasenheide**, on the northern fringe of Tempelhof Airport. Halfway along, on Marheinekeplatz, are the well-stocked **Markthalle** (Market Hall) and the **Passionkirche**; another red-brick structure in the area is the **Wasserturm** (Water Tower) from 1888, now a café, on neat and tidy Chamissoplatz.

Eastern Kreuzberg ★★

For an authentic taste of the Orient, take the U-Bahn to Kottbusser Tor, sidestep the rather good fruit and vegetable market, get a whiff of spicy eastern food cooking, and head down Adalbertstraße towards **Oranienstraße**, the main drag that splices Kreuzberg's eastern quarter. At its colourful heart, Kreuzberg resembles an Oriental bazaar where you can buy just about anything.

This part of Kreuzberg is sometimes known by the postal code SO36 (SO standing for *Süd-Ost*, or Southeast) that was used in the days before the five-digit codes, setting it apart from western Kreuzberg (SO61). It was in SO36 that Kreuzberg's reputation as a haven for punks, squatters and dropouts evolved – a fringe society far less in evidence today than it was in the 1980s.

An insight into the fascinating history of the district is recalled in the **Kreuzberg Museum**, housed in a disused factory at Adalbertstraße 95, among the unattractive apartment blocks around Kottbusser Tor U-Bahn station. Open Wednesday–Sunday 12:00–18:00. A short way south of Kottbusser Tor, on Maybachufer – the south bank of the Landwehrkanal – the atmospheric open-air **Turkish Market** takes place on Tuesday and Friday afternoons. There is no better place for experiencing the sights, sounds and smells of the Orient this side of Istanbul.

Above: *One of the many Turkish eateries to be found in Berlin.*

PROTEST POINT

Kreuzberg became a focus of **anti-American rioting** in 1987 and was effectively sealed off from the rest of Berlin for a visit by US President **Ronald Reagan** to celebrate the city's 750th anniversary. Buildings were burned, cars wrecked and shops boarded up across the district, where unemployment had reached record levels. Reagan's plea to the East – echoing Kennedy's words almost a quarter-century earlier – for the Wall to be torn down fell on deaf Soviet ears at the time; two years later the border was opened.

Above: *Smart apartments in Prenzlauer Berg.*

RENT BARRACKS

Mietskasernen (literally 'rent barracks') was the name given to the rows of five-storey tenement blocks dating from the late 19th century that still characterize parts of **Kreuzberg** and **Prenzlauer Berg**. The buildings were linked by deep inner court-yards – into which the sun rarely, if ever, shone – and reached back several blocks from the street. In the most spartan living conditions, up to eight people would share a single room in which they lived, ate, slept, and often also worked to supplement a meagre income.
At the turn of the century, a quarter of Berlin's population dwelt in *Mietskasernen*.

PRENZLAUER BERG

Like Kreuzberg, the inner suburb northeast of the centre that the locals call Prenzl'berg was jammed up against the Wall, its crowded tenement buildings suffering from neglect and the whole area distinctly run-down. Similarly, since the Wall was removed, much of this one-time working-class district has been given a facelift. It now houses a large **student** population and is among Berlin's more fashionable eating and drinking areas, sporting cafés, restaurants and the delightful watering holes the Germans call *Kneipen*.

Using Senefelderplatz U-Bahn station as a starting point – the square was named after Alois Senefelder, who invented lithography – the **Jüdischer Friedhof** (Jewish Cemetery) is a short way north on Schönhauser Allee. It has been in use since 1827, having replaced the Old Jewish Cemetery on Grosse Hamburger Straße. Here rest the painter Max Liebermann (1847–1935), publisher Leopold Ullstein (1826–99) and composer Giacomo Meyerbeer (1791–864). The cemetery, which suffered at the Nazis' hands in World War II, is open Monday–Thursday 08:00–16:00, Friday 8:00–13:00. Male visitors are requested to keep their heads covered.

Kollwitzplatz ★★

Beyond the cemetery up Schönhauser Allee, the brick-built **Segenskirche** squashed up between apartment buildings on the left dates from 1906. Straight ahead, Schönhauser Allee becomes the main shopping street in this part of the city, its shops fronting an elevated section of U-Bahn that pops up in the middle of the road. Turning right on Wörther Straße brings you to the three-cornered **Kollwitzplatz**, named after the Berlin artist Käthe Kollwitz following her death in 1945. This is the heart of the 'new' Prenzlauer Berg; the green park in the middle of the square contains Gustav Seitz's outsize statue of the artist in her later years seated on a drab concrete plinth. Käthe Kollwitz's sympathetic portrayals of

Left: *Kollwitzplatz, with its restored buildings and expanding restaurant and nightlife scene, is at the heart of Prenzlauer Berg*

the working-class people of Prenzlauer Berg among whom she lived and worked for 50 years earned her a place in their hearts. Many of her works are displayed in the Käthe Kollwitz Museum on Fasanenstraße in Charlottenburg (*see* page 70).

Beyond Kollwitzplatz, Kollwitzstraße contains many freshly restored buildings; the area has undergone a thorough facelift. A model for the district is **Husemannstraße**, a street restored to its turn-of-the-century elegance by the GDR as a spruced-up showpiece for Berlin's 750th

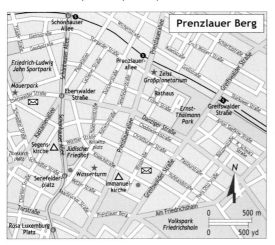

PRENZL'BERG WALK

This short walk takes you around the heart of the Prenzlauer Berg district:
• Take the **U-Bahn** to **Senefelderplatz**.
• Turn right up the wide Schönhauser Allee to the **Jüdischer Friedhof** (Jewish Cemetery).
• Continue past the cemetery and take the first turning right into Wörther Straße. Proceed to **Kollwitzplatz**.
• Midway along the north side of the park at *Restauration 1900*, turn left into **Husemannstraße**.
• The first right into Sredzkistraße and then right again into Kollwitzstraße returns you to Kollwitzplatz.
• At the southern tip of the square turn left into **Knaackstraße**.
• Turn right past the **Wasserturm** (Water Tower), and then turn left at the end to emerge on wide **Prenzlauer Allee**.
• Catch a **tram** back to Hackescher Markt.

TRIPS BY TRAM

It is fair to say that had Berlin not been partitioned after World War II, there would probably be no trams running in the city today. While tramlines in the former **West Berlin** were ripped up in the 1960s, the **East Berlin** authorities – as in other GDR cities like **Leipzig** and **Dresden** – maintained their tram system, albeit with ageing tramcars. Since reunification of the city, the network has been **updated** and today modern yellow trams run over the 30 lines serving the eastern suburbs. Plans to reintroduce trams in some parts of the western city have yet to be realized.

Below: *Prenzlauer Berg's Water Tower has been converted into flats; the Nazis used it as a torture chamber.*

anniversary celebrations in 1987; even the street signs have an antique appearance. The effort is now being repeated in neighbouring streets to good effect. The area around Kollwitzplatz, along Kollwitzstraße and into Knaackstraße is packed with restaurants and makes an excellent alternative to longer-established eating out areas of the city.

Just south of Kollwitzplatz is a Prenzl'berg landmark – the fat, yellow-brick **Wasserturm** (Water Tower) on Knaackstraße, built in 1875. In use until 1915, it was taken over by the Nazis, who turned its basement into an interrogation and torture chamber. Now it is an oddly shaped apartment house – a protected building with a memorial stone that pays tribute to freedom fighters killed by the Nazis in 1933. To the north of the water tower at Rykestraße 53 is the only Berlin synagogue to have survived the war.

About 500m (550yd) west of the Eberswalder Straße U-Bahn station, at the confluence of Bernauer Straße and Eberswalder Straße, is the **Mauerpark** – a lengthy section of the Wall that has been sprayed and resprayed by graffiti artists to document events since 1989. The former **Todesstreifen** (Death Strip) alongside the Wall has been greened over. About 1.5km (0.9 mile) north along the line of the Wall from here is the site of the Bornholmer Straße **border crossing**; it was here, momentously, on 9 November 1989 that East Berliners were first allowed access to the West. Another section of Wall can be seen at the **Gedenkstätte Berliner Mauer**, a memorial at the western end of Bernauerstraße, close to Nordbahnhof S-Bahn station, in combination with border installations.

Prenzlauer Berg's own green open space is 1km (0.5 mile) northeast of Kollwitzplatz, in **Ernst-Thälmann-Park**, named after the early communist leader murdered by the Nazis. Here is the **Zeiss Großplanetarium**, a multimedia attraction that covers a range of astronomical subjects, accompanied by music and lasers.

Left: *Berlin boasts a wealth of bookshops covering a wide variety of subjects.*

LICHTENBERG

The suburb of Lichtenberg lies beyond Freidrichshain, to the southeast of the city centre. Here is Berlin's second zoo, the **Tierpark Friedrichsfelde**, covering some 160ha (395 acres) and boasting a collection of 8000 animals of almost 1000 species drawn from five continents. Built by the GDR in 1955 for East Berliners to rival West Berlin's Zoologischer Garten in Charlottenburg, the Tierpark Friedrichsfelde ranks among the largest zoos in Europe. It occupies grounds that once belonged to the Baroque **Schloß Friedrichsfelde** (Friedrichsfelde Palace), which was completed in 1695; nowadays concerts are staged there. Open daily 09:00–19:00/dusk.

Approximately 2km (1 mile) southeast of the zoo, in the adjacent suburb of Karlshorst, is the **Museum Berlin-Karlshorst**. This was the place where the German Wehrmacht signed its unconditional surrender on the night of 8 May 1945, officially bringing World War II to an end in Europe. The museum reopened in 1995 and contains an exhibit highlighting German-Soviet relations from 1917 until reunification. It is situated at Zwieseler Straße 4, at the junction with Rheinsteinstraße, about 1km (0.5 mile) from Karlshorst S-Bahn. Open Tuesday–Sunday 10:00–18:00.

Close to Magdalenenstraße U-Bahn station is the **Stasi Museum**, examining the history of communist East Germany and the organizations that persecuted its citi-

A GOOD READ

Head for Savignyplatz if you are looking for a decent selection of **bookshops**. Among the top stores are:

• **Autorenbuchhandlung**, at Carmerstraße 10 (strong on poetry and literature; authors occasionally give readings).

• **Bücherbogen**, at S-Bahnbogen 593, Savignyplatz (illustrated books; specialists in architecture, visual arts and design).

• **Marga Schoeller**, at Knesebeckstraße 33 (a good selection, known for its books on film).

• **Romanische Buchhandlung**, at Knesebeckstraße 20 (works grounded on Latin-based languages).

• **Galerie 2000**, Knesebeckstrasse 56-58

• Nearby, at Tauentzienstraße 13, is **Hugendubel**, with four floors of books and a café.

Right: *The replica Liberty Bell in Schöneberg Town Hall was a gift from the US Government.*

Opposite: *The 20m (65ft) Airlift Memorial, erected at Tempelhof in 1951 in memory of those who died during the Berlin Airlift.*

THE GAY CITY

Berlin's reputation as the European centre of the gay lifestyle dates from the 1920s, when clubs like the Eldorado and Kleist-Casino were venues for the city's gay and lesbian groups. Today more than 100 **gay bars** flourish in Berlin, many of them around Nollendorfplatz in Schöneberg, a few blocks south of the Tiergarten; among the more popular gay bars are Lenz, Hafen, Anderes Ufer and Eldorado. Berlin's large gay population suffered persecution under the Nazis and a considerable number were dispatched to concentration camps – a triangular **plaque** in the wall outside Nollendorfplatz U-Bahn station recalls their plight.

zens. Housed in the former headquarters of the East German state security police (Stasi) at Ruschestraße 103, the centre contains photographs, documents, victims' reports, surveillance equipment and the office of the last Stasi chief, Erich Mielke. Open Monday–Friday 11:00–18:00, Saturday–Sunday 14:00–18:00.

SCHÖNEBERG

The name of this southern district means 'beautiful mountain' – in reality a small rise atop which sits the imposing **Rathaus Schöneberg** (Schöneberg Town Hall) on Martin-Luther-Straße. From its steps, US President John F Kennedy made his famous speech to the people of Berlin in June 1963 (*see* box, opposite page); after Kennedy's murder on 22 November that year, the square in front was renamed in his honour. The building was completed in 1914; in its 70m (230ft) tower is the **Liberty Bell**, a replica of the famous Philadelphia original, that was presented by the US Government in 1950. The Rathaus Schöneberg served as West Berlin's Town Hall up to 1990, when the city's administration became centralized in the Red Town Hall (*see* page 47).

Located about 2km (1 mile) northeast of the Rathaus is the Kleistpark, a former botanical garden taking the name of the Romantic poet, Heinrich von Kleist. At the entrance to the park along Potsdamer Straße are the

Königskolonnaden (Royal Colonnades) of 1780, the work of Karl von Gontard, who designed the domes of the French and German Cathedrals on Gendarmenmarkt (*see* page 38). They were moved to their present site from Alexanderplatz in 1910, when the **Kammergericht** (Supreme Court of Justice) was being built within the park. This was later to become the Nazi People's Court, where political opponents received their show trial and were sent for execution, usually in Plötzensee prison. After the war the building stood empty for much of the time, but since 1990 it has again been used by the Supreme Court.

Just to the north of here is **Winterfeldplatz**, the setting for an excellent twice-weekly market and the towering **St Matthias-Kirche**.

Nearby **Nollendorfplatz**, another two blocks north, was a hub of Berlin nightlife and the centre of the city's gay community in the 1920s and 1930s – a period from which the **Metropol**, built in 1906, survives. It now houses the Goya nightclub for up to 1500 revellers with its huge dance floor, lounges, cocktail bars, restaurant and female bouncers. At Nollendorfstraße 17 lived British author Christopher Isherwood, whose tales of the city in *Goodbye to Berlin* were the inspiration behind the film *Cabaret*.

TEMPELHOF

Bounded by Schöneberg to the west and Kreuzberg to the north, Tempelhof is the site of the former military **airport** that kept Berlin going through the Berlin Airlift of 1948–49. It was once Germany's largest airport; today it handles mostly domestic traffic and with the development of Schönefeld as Berlin's leading airport it is scheduled to close in October 2008. At Tempelhof's entrance is the **Luftbrückendenkmal** (Airlift Memorial) to the 78 air crew and service staff who died in the operation.

SWEET TALK

With the Wall in place, visiting US president **John F Kennedy** made his famous Cold War speech from the steps of the **Rathaus Schöneberg** in June 1963. His speech concluded with the immortal words: 'All free men, wherever they may live, are citizens of Berlin, and therefore, as a free man, I take pride in the words "*Ich bin ein Berliner*".' What Kennedy's scriptwriters had not appreciated was that to Berlin's citizens, 'Berliner' is a popular shortened version of *Berliner Pfannkuchen*. Their leader had thus informed his host city: 'I am a doughnut.'

7
The Outer Suburbs

Berlin's outer suburbs contain much of interest to the visitor and are easily accessible from the city centre by U-Bahn or S-Bahn trains – they can provide a refreshingly welcome break from doing the rounds of the city centre sights. Before 1989, the rivers and lakes of Spandau and Wannsee provided the only recreational areas for West Berliners.

SPANDAU

For many, the name Spandau still conjures up memories of Hitler's deputy, **Rudolf Hess**, languishing for years in the Allied War Criminals jail associated with Berlin's northwest suburb before committing suicide there in 1987 – at the end of his life he was the jail's sole occupant. The jail on Wilhelmstraße, some 4km (2.5 miles) from Spandau's centre, has long been demolished – today's visitors come to see Spandau's fine 16th-century citadel, amble through the streets of the Old Town or enjoy a boat ride on the river.

Spandau Zitadelle ★★

Spandau's strategic position at the confluence of the Spree and Havel rivers demanded protection – and it was provided from the 12th century by an early citadel fortress. Work began on a replacement Zitadelle in 1560 and the square fortress was completed in the Italian Renaissance style some 34 years later. Above the splendid gateway off Straße Am Juliusturm is the Hohenzollern coat of arms. Four **bastions** jut out into the moat, and in

---

DON'T MISS

★★ Spandau Zitadelle: Renaissance-style fortress in the green hinterland.
★★ Old Spandau: contains Berlin's oldest house.
★★ Dahlem museums: big complex in the district of Zehlendorf.
★ Glienicker Bridge: where the Cold War spy exchanges took place.

Opposite: *Spandau's fine 16th-century Citadel is scenically located at the meeting point of the Spree and Havel rivers.*

CHRISTMAS MARKETS

Visit Berlin just before
Christmas and the aroma of
mulled wine, candied almonds
and cinnamon cakes is never
far away: this is the season
when *Weihnachtsmärkte*
(Christmas markets) spring up
all over the city, their attrac-
tively decorated stalls packed
with seasonal offerings. One of
the most attractive Christmas
markets takes place on the
Gendarmenmarkt; the largest is
in the Altstadt (old town) of
Spandau, out to the northwest.
Other markets are held by the
**Kaiser Wilhelm Memorial
Church** at **Alexanderplatz**, on
Unter den Linden and in
Sophienstraße on the edge of
the Scheunenviertel.

the southwest corner of the inner courtyard is the 36m
(118ft) **Juliusturm** (Julius Tower) – climb the 145 steps for
outstanding views. An exhibit on the citadel's history can
be found in the **Kommandantenhaus** (commander's
house), and the Spandau Local History Museum has set
itself up in the former **Zeughaus** (armoury). The fortress
is 300m (328yd) west of Zitadelle U-Bahn station.
Open Tuesday–Friday 09:00–17:00, Saturday–Sunday
10:00–17:00.

Old Spandau ★★

Spandau is older than Berlin itself and was only incorporated into the city in 1920. The mostly pedestrianized
Altstadt (Old Town), a few minutes' walk west of the
Zitadelle, contains some interesting buildings, oldest
among them the 15th-century **Gotisches Haus** (Gothic
House) at Breite Straße 32 – first turning on your left
across the Havel bridge. During restoration work, foundations of a 13th-century town house were discovered in its
basement – it is Berlin's oldest residential building.

On Reformationsplatz is the elegant 15th-century
Nikolaikirche. Its treasures include a bronze baptismal
font from 1398, a late-Renaissance altar from 1582 and a
Baroque pulpit of 1714. The statue before the red-brick
tower is of the Brandenburg leader Elector Joachim II,
whose conversion to Lutheranism in 1539 sparked the
Reformation that spread throughout the March of
Brandenburg. From a corner of the square next to the
church, Mönchstraße leads
to the **Marktplatz**, with its
lively market.

On the northern side
of Straße Am Juliusturm
is the part of the Altstadt
often referred to as **Kolk**,
though this is but one of
several narrow cobbled
lanes that make up the
Behnitz locality. The small
church at its heart is the

Opposite: *Wannsee provides weekend relaxation
for thousands of Berliners.*

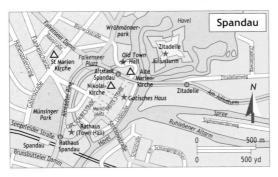

Marienkirche (St Mary's Church), which dates from 1848 but was rebuilt after suffering World War II damage. On Behnitz there is a brightly painted **Feuermelde** (fire alarm post); on Hoher Steinweg is a surviving 70m (77yd) stretch of Spandau's 14th-century **town wall**.

The lock just east of the Behnitz area, opened in 1910, connects the upper and lower sections of the Havel River. From here you can travel by boat to the centre of Berlin, Treptow, Wannsee and Potsdam.

WANNSEE

Wannsee is situated at the heart of the southwest lakes district, between the lakes Grosser Wannsee and Kleiner Wannsee and, with its elegant villas and houses of the well-to-do, is unquestionably one of the most desirable parts of Berlin in which to live. The town itself stretches to the south along the edge of two smaller lakes, Pohlesee and Stölpchensee.

On the edge of Kleiner Wannsee a **memorial stone** marks the spot where the 19th-century Romantic poet Heinrich von Kleist shot his incurably sick mistress, Henriette Vogel, and then committed suicide in 1811.

Overlooking the larger lake, at Am Grossen Wannsee 58, is the **Haus der Wannsee Konferenz** (Wannsee Conference Building), an exclusive villa in which Nazi leaders planned the mass extermination of European Jews in January 1942, in what became known as the Final Solution. A permanent exhibit of documents and photographs covering the Holocaust recalls this bleakest chapter in German history. It is open daily 10:00–18:00 (except public holidays).

Boat trips operate from Wannsee to **Pfaueninsel** (Peacock Island), where Friedrich Wilhelm II had a small folly built for his mistress Wilhelmine Encke in 1794–97; within it is a small museum.

GLIENICKE BRIDGE

The dull green metal bridge near the Schloß Glienicke, linking Berlin with Potsdam, today carries traffic in Berlin's extreme southwest, but it was not always so. Closed throughout the **Cold War** years, when the East-West border followed the **Havel River** below, this was the scene of **spy swaps** between the Americans and Russians. Here, in 1962, shot-down American U2 pilot **Gary Powers** found his way back to the West in exchange for a Soviet agent; the bridge thus became a symbol of the Cold War and featured in spy films and novels.

Right: *The Botanical Garden at Dahlem is one of the largest of its kind in the world.*

DAHLEM

The Zehlendorf suburb of Dahlem is best known for the **Dahlem Museum Complex**. An excursion to this southerly district is a cultural delight – it contains the **Ethnologisches Museum** (Ethnological Museum) and **Museum Europäischer Kulturen** (Museum of European Cultures), both close to Dahlem-Dorf U-Bahn station. The Ethnological Museum has much to interest observers of non-European culture – there are superb collections from Early America, Africa, South and East Asia and the South Pacific, including Australia. The other museum focuses on everyday culture in Germany and elsewhere in Europe, with a fascinating collection from the 18th century. Open Tuesday–Friday 10:00–18:00, Saturday–Sunday 11:00–18:00.

TREPTOW

Millions of Berliners and countless visitors to the city have descended on the southeast district of Treptow since the **Treptower Park** was laid out by Gustav Meyer alongside the River Spree in the 1880s and 1890s. In the centre of the 78ha (193-acre) park, the **Sowjetisches Ehrenmal** (Soviet Monument), erected between 1946 and 1949, commemorates 5000 of the Red Army soldiers killed in the Battle of Berlin in April–May 1945 – they are buried close by. The site contains a mausoleum, an 11m (36ft) high monument – it depicts a Soviet soldier carrying a child, his sword resting on a broken swastika – and memorial plaques. It is reached through an archway off the southern side of Puschkinallee.

ANNA SEGHERS

Communist authoress Anna Seghers, born **Netty Reiling** in 1900, settled in Berlin after World War II exile in **Mexico**, during which time she produced *The Seventh Cross*, a profound work that chronicled life in Nazi Germany. The small apartment in the former East Berlin in which she lived and worked now contains a **literary workshop** of her life, complete with her small **library**. It is at Anna-Seghers-Straße 81 in Treptow, named in her honour following her death in 1983. Open Tuesday and Thursday 10:00–16:00.

KÖPENICK

The locals think of Köpenick, on the southeast edge of Berlin, as the real 'back of beyond'. Among the largest of Berlin's districts, with its woods and waterways it is far more rural retreat than suburban city. In Grosser Müggelsee, 4km (2.5 miles) by 2.5km (1.5 miles), it boasts Berlin's largest lake, and in the 115m (377ft) Müggelberge the city's highest hill. It also has the 17th-century **Schloß Köpenick** (Köpenick Palace), with its division of the Kunstgewerbemuseum (Decorative Arts Museum).

PANKOW

The chief attraction in the northern district of Pankow is the **Schloß Niederschönhausen**, a former residence of the GDR head of state and later a GDR government 'guesthouse' for visiting dignitaries who included Soviet leader Mikhail Gorbachev. Built as a manor house in 1664, it was enlarged in the early 18th century; the surrounding Schloßpark is the work of Peter Lenne. In Pankow's town centre are the neo-Baroque **Rathaus** (town hall) and 15th-century parish church.

WEISSENSEE

To the east of Pankow and north of Prenzlauer Berg, Weissensee is named after the near-circular **Weisser See** (white lake) alongside Berliner Allee. It is a highly popular picnic spot, good for boating and basking in the sun. The Jüdischer Friedhof Weissensee is one of Europe's largest Jewish cemeteries. It opened in 1880, taking over when from the cemetery at Schönhauser Alle had been filled to capacity. Male visitors should cover their heads – you can borrow a skullcap.

CAPTAIN DESPERATE

The best-known figure in Köpenick history is **Wilhelm Voigt**, a down-and-out shoemaker whose bronze statue stands in front of the neo-Gothic town hall. Desperate to improve his lot but lacking authorization to leave the city, Voigt donned a captain's uniform and with some passing soldiers stormed into the town hall and plundered the coffers. German writer **Carl Zuckmayer** immortalized the incident in his play *Der Hauptmann von Köpenick* (The Captain of Köpenick), written in 1931; his plays were later banned by the Nazis.

Below: *The Soviet Monument in Treptower Park commemorates soldiers who died in the Battle of Berlin.*

SAINT BENEDICT LIBRARY
DUFFIELD ROAD
DERBY
DE22 1JD

8
Around Berlin

Those with some time to spare on a visit to Berlin would do very well to explore the **Brandenburg** surrounds, and perhaps head south to take in **Dresden** or **Leipzig**. There are many places of interest within a short distance of the capital: **Potsdam** is but a short S-bahn ride away, Brandenburg some 60km (37 miles) distant and the **Spreewald**, with its 400km (250 miles) of waterways, upwards of 80km (50 miles) to the southeast. Near Oranienburg, 35km (22 miles) to the northwest of Berlin, the former **Sachsenhausen Concentration Camp** is a sobering memorial.

POTSDAM

For almost three decades, the Wall separated western Berlin from its immediate and older neighbour. The Brandenburg capital is only 24km (15 miles) from central Berlin and with excellent rail connections (S-Bahn to Potsdam Stadt), it makes a thoroughly worthwhile day trip – or even an extension of two or three days. The chief attraction, **Sanssouci Park** with its palaces and pavilions, lies immediately west of the Old Town; some 3km (2 miles) northeast is the **Schloß Cecilienhof**, scene of the 1945 Potsdam Conference.

Schloß Sanssouci **

The Sanssouci Palace is Potsdam's showpiece, designed in 1747 by **Georg von Knobelsdorff** as a summer country retreat for Friedrich II (**Frederick the Great**). 'Sanssouci' translates into the 18th-century equivalent of 'no worries'

DON'T MISS

** **Schloß Sanssouci:** showpiece palace and park in the centre of Potsdam.
** **Sachsenhausen:** memorial site of the Nazis' concentration camp.
** **Brandenburg:** some fine old buildings in its old town.
* **Schloß Cecilienhof:** the scene of the 1945 Potsdam Conference.
* **Babelsberg Film Studios:** a centre of Germany's film industry.
* **Kloster Chorin:** a monastery staging open-air summer concerts.

Opposite: *The ornate gateway to the show-piece Schloß Sanssouci.*

POTSDAM CONFERENCE

The ivy-clad walls, half-timbered exterior and Tudor chimney stacks give an unexpected air of familiarity to the **Schloß Cecilienhof**, designed as an English country manor house for **Kaiser Wilhelm II** in the early 1900s. Here at the Potsdam Conference in July and August 1945, **Winston Churchill** (replaced in mid-conference by **Clement Attlee**), **Harry S Truman** and **Josef Stalin** met to settle the postwar division of Germany that was to last 45 years; the conference chamber, with its large table and the rooms used by the three delegations, can be visited. Open April–October 09:00–17:00, November–March 09:00–16:00, closed Monday.

and there could be no better name for a building that provided such perfect relaxation away from the cares of state. The single-storey Rococo palace is surmounted by a green dome; behind it, wide steps lead down through a steeply terraced vineyard and past an array of sculptures to the **Great Fountain** and small **lake**. Among the collection of opulent rooms within the palace are the stunning **Konzertsaal** (Concert Hall), the impressive **Marmorsaal** (Marble Hall) and the **Voltaire Zimmer**, named after the French philosopher, a frequent guest, and decorated with colourful birds. The palace suffered from a fair amount of neglect under the GDR administration, but since 1990 has regained its former glory with a place among UNESCO's World Heritage Sites. Open Tuesday–Sunday 09:00–17:00 in April–October, 09:00–16:00 in November–March.

Sanssouci Park ★★

The Schloß Sanssouci has pride of place in the massive Sanssouci Park, which covers some 300ha (741 acres) and stretches a good 2km (1 mile) from the centre of Potsdam. The park's splendid array of other buildings includes the **Bildergalerie** (Picture Gallery), purpose-built in 1764 and containing works of masters including Rubens, Caravaggio and Van Dyck; it is situated just east of the palace. On the western side is the **Neue Kammern** (New Chambers), now used as a guesthouse; about 500m (550yd) southwest of the palace is the delight-

Below: *The attractive Chinese Tea House at Schloß Sanssouci.*

ful **Chinesisches Teehaus** (Chinese Tea House), from 1757, its circular roof supported by gilded palm trees and bearing a gilded Mandarin. West of the palace are the **Orangerie**, a Renaissance-style building of 1864 that accommodated visiting royalty, and also the **Sizilianischer Garten** (Sicilian Garden), complete with subtropical plants. In the south of the park is the **Schloß Charlottenhof**, built in 1826 by Karl Friedrich Schinkel.

Neues Palais ★★

Built by Friedrich II as a symbol of Prussian might in the aftermath of the successful Seven Years' War, the red-brick Neues Palais (New Palace) with its huge **green dome** was an extra-vagant Rococo addition to the park in 1769. The exterior design was the work of **Johann Büring**, while the interior was styled by **Karl von Gontard**. A few of the palace's 200 or so rooms are on view to the public (open daily, except Friday; hours as for Schloß Sanssouci). For the best view of the Neues Palais, approach from the east down its long drive. Behind the palace are the two Rococo-styled **Communs**, linked by a curving façade and built to house the palace staff.

Above: *Steps lead down through the terraced vine-yards in the grounds of Schloß Sanssouci.*

Altstadt ★

Though the palaces and parks provide the chief reason for a visit to Potsdam, do not overlook the **Altstadt** (Old Town), with its superb collection of 18th-century buildings. Pedestrianized **Brandenburger Straße**, Potsdam's principal shopping street, connects the Luisenplatz at its western end with the Bassinplatz, where a couple of historic churches are located – the **Französische Kirche** (French Church), built for the Huguenot community in 1753, and also the

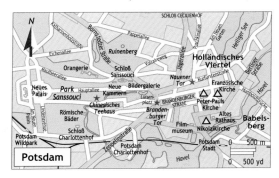

Peter-Pauls-Kirche from 1868. North of Bassinplatz, the **Holländisches Viertel** (Dutch Quarter) contains many 18th-century red-brick gabled houses built for Dutch immigrant workers, some of which have been restored. On Am Alten Markt are the lovely domed **Nikolaikirche** (St Nicholas Church), built to Schinkel's neoclassical plans in 1850, and the **Altes Rathaus** (Old Town Hall) from 1753, now containing art galleries and a cellar restaurant. Another old building put to good modern use is Knobelsdorff's elegant **Marstall**, the former royal stables from the 1740s that now house the **Filmmuseum**, prominently featuring material obtained from the nearby Babelsberg Film Studios (see below).

Above: *These 18th-century gabled houses are in the Dutch Quarter of Potsdam.*

POTSDAM GATEWAYS

Potsdam boasts some fine gateways that survived the bombing of World War II. The **Brandenburger Tor** (Brandenburg Gate), constructed in 1770 on Luisenplatz, is some 20 years older than its more famous namesake in Berlin and itself is predated by the **Nauener Tor** (Nauen Gate) from 1755 north of the Old Town. Between them is the **Jägertor** (Hunter's Gate).

Babelsberg ★

Over the Havel from Potsdam lies Babelsberg, with its palace and film studios. The neo-Gothic **Schloß Babelsberg** (Babelsberg Castle) was designed by Schinkel in 1833 as a summer residence for the future Kaiser Wilhelm I. The highlight of the castle is the octagonal ballroom. Open May–October, Tuesday–Sunday 10:00–17:00.

The **Babelsberg Film Studios** on Grossbeerenstraße have earned an important place in German film history – the 40ha (100-acre) site, the studios of the former GDR film company DEFA, is among the oldest and largest of its kind in the world. Among the films shot here were *Metropolis*, by Fritz Lang; *The Blue Angel*, starring a young Marlene Dietrich; and *The Neverending Story*. The site includes the Filmpark Babelsberg, a movie theme park with guided behind-the-scenes tours, special effects exhibits and a spectacular stunt show. Open March–October, daily 10:00–18:00 (allow four hours).

BRANDENBURG

Brandenburg, 30km (19 miles) west of Potsdam, is the oldest town in the province to which it lends its name – Slavs first settled here in the 6th century – and makes a worthwhile day excursion from Berlin. Waterways split the town into the Altstadt (Old Town), Neustadt (New Town) and Dominsel (Cathedral Island). At the heart of the restored Altstadt is the 14th-century **Altes Rathaus** (Old Town Hall), with its **Roland statue** (1474), a symbol of Brandenburg's market town status; the Neustadt is dominated by the 15th-century **Katherinenkirche** (Parish Church of St Catherine). The **Dom Sts Peter und Paul** (St Peter and Paul Cathedral) on Dominsel was started in Romanesque style in 1165 and finished in Gothic style 75 years later; highlights include the **Bunte Kapelle** (Colourful Chapel) from 1235 and the **Dommuseum**, containing religious exhibits and local history.

SPREEWALD

An hour by rail southeast of Berlin brings you to **Lübben** and **Lübbenau** in the very heart of the Spreewald (Spree Forest), a scenic area crisscrossed by 400km (250 miles) of rivers and canals where a boat or punt offers one of the best ways of getting around. The region is also great for hiking and fishing, and on warm summer weekends thousands of Berliners come in their droves to overdose on rest and relaxation. The self-styled 'capital' of the region is picturesque Lübbenau.

SOUTHERN FUN

Head for Berlin's southern district of **Neukölln** for off-centre leisure venues. The **Blub Badeparadies** at Buschkrugallee 64 in Neukölln is one of Europe's most attractive and varied water parks, while the **Stadtbad Neukölln** at Ganghoferstraße 3–5 was described as Europe's most beautiful indoor swimming pool when it opened in 1914.

Left: *The market town of Brandenburg is an easy day trip from Berlin.*

FLOWER POWER

More than 20,000 plant species from all corners of the globe have a home in Berlin's luxuriant **Botanical Garden** at **Dahlem** to the southwest of the city (see page 98). Covering 43ha (106 acres), it is one of the largest in the world and contains a 'touch' garden for the visually handicapped. You can spend hours admiring the amazing displays and then increase your knowledge of the subject in the **Botanisches Museum** within the grounds, where the history of plants and their current distribution are explained. Exhibits include dioramas of different vegetation types and grain from ancient Egyptian burial sites. The garden is open daily from 09:00 until dusk.

Below: *Bertolt Brecht statue near the Berliner Ensemble theatre. The playwright spent his summers in Buckow.*

BUCKOW

The village of Buckow lies 50km (31 miles) east of Berlin, in a 200km² (77 sq mile) country park of meandering rivers, lakes and hills known as **Märkische Schweiz** (Switzerland of the March). It came to the attention of Berliners in the 1950s, when playwright **Bertolt Brecht** and actress **Helene Weigel** spent their summers away from the city in a house that has since been turned into a museum, the **Brecht-Weigel House**. The house, still with its original furnishings, is at Bertolt-Brecht-Straße 29; here Brecht wrote most of his Buckow Elegies. Open April–October, Wednesday–Friday 13:00–17:00, Saturday–Sunday 13:00–18:00 (November–March, Wednesday–Friday 10:00–12:00, 13:00–16:00, Sunday 11:00–16:00).

CHORIN

This small town 70km (43 miles) northeast of Berlin attracts thousands of visitors each year to the Cistercian monastery of **Kloster Chorin**, for the open-air classical concerts of the Chorin Musiksommer festival. The monastery, one of the oldest red-brick Gothic buildings in northern Germany, was founded in 1273 but fell into disrepair and was later saved only through **Friedrich Schinkel's** renovation efforts in the early 1800s. Open daily 09:00–18:00 (November–March, 09:00–16:00).

Niederfinow ★

Just 10km (6 miles) from Chorin is the **Schiffshebewerk Niederfinow**, a massive ship hoist used to raise or lower barges and other craft the 36m (118ft) between the Oder River and Oder-Havel Canal. Visitors can view it from a walkway by the upper canal level – open daily 09:00–18:00 (January–March, Monday–Friday 09:00–16:00, Saturday–Sunday 09:00–17:00).

SACHSENHAUSEN

The Sachsenhausen **concentration camp** set up in 1936 by the Nazis on the site of a former brewery near Oranienburg, some 35km (22 miles) northwest of Berlin, has since 1961 been a memorial to more than 100,000

Left: *Bertolt Brecht and his wife Helene Weigel are buried in the Dorotheenstädtischer Friedhof, eastern Berlin's VIP cemetery.*

prisoners who died within its walls. Two **museums** recall the horrors of life in the 'Lager', complete with film footage (definitely unsuitable for children). Two **barrack huts** have been reconstructed on the site, which also contains the **crematorium** and **Station Z extermination site**, where prisoners were executed by a shot in the back of the neck. From August 1945 until March 1950, Sachsenhausen served as a Soviet internment and disciplinary camp. Open Tuesday–Sunday 08:30–18:00 (October–March, 08:30–16:30); **archive** and **library** open Tuesday–Friday 09:00–15:30.

RHEINSBERG

Friedrich II (Frederick the Great) described the period (from 1736 to 1740) that he spent in Rheinsberg preparing to accede the throne as the happiest time of his life. The small town and its lakeside palace, **Schloß Rheinsberg** – about 90km (56 miles) north of Berlin, two hours by train – can be combined in a day trip with Sachsenhausen (*see* above). The palace on the shores of the Grienericksee took its Renaissance form in 1566; Georg von Knobelsdorff remodelled it in the 1740s for Friedrich II's brother, **Prince Heinrich**, who lived there for 60 years until he died in 1802. There is a permanent exhibition dedicated to Berlin writer **Kurt Tucholsky** (1890–1935). Open Tuesday–Sunday 10:00–17:00 (November–March, 10:00–16:00 or 17:00).

BERLIN PAST

The spirit of prewar Berlin is recaptured in **Berlin Wie es War** (Berlin As It Was) at the **Adria Filmtheater** in the southern district of **Steglitz**. At the start of the 1940s, before Berlin had been subjected to the devastating wartime Allied bombing, filmmaker **Leo de Laforgue** filmed life in the city with a simple hand-held camera; banned by **Goebbels** in 1942, the film finally reached the screen in 1950. The Adria Filmtheater is at Schloßstraße 48 in Steglitz (U-Bahn and S-Bahn, Rathaus Steglitz).

DRESDEN

An easy two-hour Autobahn trip 195km (121 miles) south of Berlin is Dresden, tagged 'the Florence of the North' centuries ago because of its splendid **architecture**. Most of Dresden's finest buildings date from the 17th century and were captured on canvas by **Canaletto**, court painter at the time of **August the Strong** of Saxony (1670–1733). But on the night of 13 February 1945, Dresden was reduced to rubble and ashes as British and American aircraft blitzed the city in one of World War II's most destructive **bombing raids** that cost some 50,000 lives; more than 60 years on, the reconstruction continues.

DRESDEN CHINA

You can buy it in dedicated Berlin shops on the **Ku'damm** and along **Unter den Linden** – the attractive porcelain bearing the blue crossed-swords trademark that identifies it as Dresden china. If you take an out-of-town excursion to Dresden you can also visit the factory in Talstraße, Meissen (more fully the **Staatliche Porzellan-Manufaktur Meissen**). Guided tours of the **workshops** show the complete production process, but expect long queues at this most popular attraction in summer. Displays in the **Schauhalle** show how porcelain styles have changed through the years.

Zwinger and Semperoper ★★

First-time visitors to Dresden should head immediately for Theaterplatz to see two of the city's finest creations – the Zwinger (Festival Square) and Semperoper (Semper Opera House), both destroyed in the war and rebuilt in their original style. The **Zwinger**, built from 1710–28 out of Saxony sandstone and designed by **Matthaeus Pöppelmann**, is regarded as a Baroque masterpiece – a large square, part-surrounded by a single-storey gallery linking the pavilions and ornate gateways. Note the **Glockenspielpavillon** in the southwest corner, where a carillon of 40 Meissen porcelain bells hangs either side of the blue clock. Museums and galleries in the Zwinger include the Old Masters Gallery, Armoury (Rüstkammer), Mathematics Salon, Porcelain Collection and Zoological Museum. The original **Semperoper**, named after Dresden's leading 19th-century architect **Gottfried Semper**, dates from 1841; the present rebuild was completed in 1985.

Another casualty of the 1945 bombing was the neo-Renaissance **Residenzschloß** (Residential Palace). A massive and costly rebuild has restored several museums to the building, with the **Grünes Gewölbe** (the Green Vault) of jewel-studded treasures returned there from the **Albertinum** museum complex, a former arsenal which also houses the New Masters Gallery.

On Neumarkt is the **Frauenkirche** (Church of Our Lady), now restored to its former glory as Germany's largest Protestant church, largely with donations from German and international foundations. On Augustus-straße, the **Verkehrsmuseum** (Transport Museum) showcases everything from old-fashioned bicycles to the very latest trains and cars. Along the southern bank of the Elbe, the raised **Brühlsche Terrasse** (Brühl Terrace) promenade offers grand views of the Neustadt and the gilded **Goldener Reiter** (Golden Rider) statue of August the Strong.

Historic Centre ★

South of Neumarkt across Wilsdruffer Straße is the **Altmarkt**, Dresden's historic core, with the rebuilt **Kreuzkirche** (Church of the Holy Cross) from 1792. Immediately behind the church is the **Neues Rathaus** (New Town Hall) of 1910.

There are more museums across the Augustusbrücke in the redeveloped Neustadt area, where reconstructed patrician houses line the pleasantly leafy Hauptstraße pedestrian precinct with its plane trees, sculptures and fountains. This is where you will find the **Museum der Frühromantik** (Museum of Early Romanticism) and also the **Staatliches Museum für Volkerkunde** (Ethnological Museum).

DRESDEN'S CASTLES

Two Baroque castles survive on the edge of Dresden. **Schloß Pillnitz** contains the neoclassical **Neues Schloß** and two summer palaces in Oriental design by Matthaeus Daniel Pöppelmann – the **Wasserpalais** and **Bergpalais**. **Schloß Moritzburg**, 15km (9.5 miles) north of Dresden, was rebuilt in the 1720s to designs by Pöppelmann, and strongly resembles a Loire chateau.

Opposite: *The Zwinger is Dresden's showpiece.*
Below: *The Semperoper, rebuilt after the war.*

LURE OF LEIPZIG

World-class composers and performers are attracted to Leipzig's **Gewandhaus**, once described by **Sir Yehudi Menuhin** as a 'temple of music'. It is worth the trip (just a couple of hours from Berlin) to take in a performance at the city's major **concert and jazz venue**. Built in 1981, it has acquired a reputation for its impressive architecture and outstanding acoustics; it is now home to the **Gewandhausorchester** under **Riccardo Chailly**. Another Leipzig venue is the **Krystallpalast Varieté**, a variety club given over to musical, dance and theatrical performances.

Opposite: *Leipzig's Nikolaikirche was a rallying point for protest against the GDR regime.*
Right: *Germany is famed for its high-quality brass band music.*
Overleaf: *The neo-Baroque Splendid Hotel on Dorotheenstraße is now an office building.*

LEIPZIG

Leipzig's origins go back 1000 years, but the city's name is firmly etched on recent history as the focus of peaceful protest by tens of thousands of GDR citizens that was seen as a prelude to the toppling of the Wall. The citizens of Leipzig, 181km (113 miles) south of Berlin, played a leading role in the **democratic revolution** of 1989 and, in October of that year, they organized demonstration marches against the GDR's dictatorship. A mass rally on 9 October was followed a week later by an estimated 120,000 taking to Leipzig's streets in a demonstration the like of which had not been seen before. The GDR government capitulated and within a month the Wall had collapsed. The elections that followed led to the **reunification** of Germany.

The Old Town ★

Most of Leipzig's historic buildings are clustered in the **Altstadt**, within the ring road that follows the line of the old city wall. At its heart is the cobbled **Marktplatz**, with the magnificent Renaissance **Altes Rathaus** (Old Town Hall) of 1556 taking up the whole of the square's eastern side; there are shops at ground floor level and the **Leipzig History Museum** on the first floor.

Behind the town hall is the **Alte Börse** of 1687, now a cultural centre with a monument to Goethe, who studied law at nearby **Leipzig University**. The University fronts Augustusplatz, the focus of the city's cultural and

academic life; on the square's northern side is the **Opernhaus**, a neoclassical creation of the communists from 1960, and on its southern edge the **Neues Gewandhaus**, the city's major concert and jazz venue.

Between the Marktplatz and University is the **Nikolaikirche** (St Nicholas Church), its exterior a blend of Gothic and Romanesque styles dating from the mid-1100s and the interior a combination of Rococo and neoclassical, the product of a late 18th-century redesign. The church was a rallying point for peaceful protests from May 1989. West of the Marktplatz along Thomasgasse you will find the **Thomaskirche** (Church of St Thomas), where **Johann Sebastian Bach** was in charge of the music from 1723 until his death in 1750; he is buried next to the altar.

Leipzig's Museums ★

Directly opposite the church, the **Bach Museum** contains pictures and documents relating to the composer's time in Leipzig, where he penned some of his best-known works. Other interesting museums in Leipzig include the **Stasi Museum** (state secret police) at Dittrichring 24, north of the Thomaskirche, and the **Ägyptisches Museum**, which displays some 9000 items and is one of Europe's most important Egyptian collections. The University's newly renovated Art Deco **Grassi** complex at Johannisplatz houses the **Musikinstrumenten Museum** (Musical Instruments Museum), the **Museum für Völkerkunde** (Ethnological Museum) and the **Museum für Angewandte Kunst** (Museum of Applied Arts).

BATTLE LINES

The massive stone **Battle of Nations monument** outside Leipzig's city centre recalls **Napoleon's defeat** by the combined armies of Prussia, Austria and Russia in the 1813 Battle of Nations – a key conflict in European history that played an important part in determining today's national boundaries. It stands 91m (300ft) high and offers superb **views of Leipzig** and its surrounds.

Berlin at a Glance

BEST TIMES TO VISIT

Berlin has a continental climate of extremes, which generally means very hot summers and freezing cold winters; **spring** and **autumn** are pleasant in-between seasons. If you can choose when to visit Berlin, try to avoid the winter months of January and February, when the bitingly cold east wind sweeping across the North European Plain numbs both the skin and the senses. Though December is also usually cold, the **Christmas markets** are a big attraction, and a warming glass or two of Glühwein will go some way towards compensating for the outside chill.

From **April–October** is the best time to go to Berlin – preferably in April, May, September and October if you want to avoid taking the chance of catching a mid-summer heatwave. However, with its expansive inner-city parklands and the beautiful lakes along its fringes, Berlin is a city that is able to breathe and even the high summer days are seldom too un-bearably hot to preclude sightseeing. The months of June to September are ideal for strolling around in the Tiergarten, taking a boat trip on the Spree, people-watching from an outdoor café on the Ku'damm, or simply getting out of town to enjoy the lakes.

GETTING THERE

As the new federal capital of Germany, Berlin is well served by **flights** from most of the European capitals and in-creasingly from points much further afield. From the UK, British Airways and low-cost airlines offer direct services from London and provide connections for travellers without direct flights. You can now fly direct to Berlin from around 200 airports in 70 countries. Some 80 airlines use Berlin's three **airports** – Tegel, Schönefeld and Tempelhof. **Tegel**, formerly West Berlin's main airport 8km (5 miles) north of the city centre, handles mainly traffic from western Europe. British Airways flies from Heathrow to Tegel, which has its own Autobahn link to the city. Buses connect the airport with U-Bahn stations – 109 and X9 go to Jakob-Kaiser-Platz and 128 to Kurt-Schuhmacher-Platz. On Berlin's southeastern fringe, 20km (12 miles) from the centre, the former East Berlin airport of **Schönefeld** handles primarily low-cost airlines and also serves east-ern Europe and Asia. The red double-decker Airport Express train, which operates from 04:30–23:00, takes 30 min-utes into central Berlin; a free shuttle bus operates to the air-port station. Schönefeld is to become Berlin's sole inter-national airport, with a much-expanded terminal and passenger handling capability – the opening of Berlin Brandeburg International is scheduled for 2011.

Driving to Berlin along Europe's comprehensive motorway network on to the Berliner Ring Autobahn that surrounds the city is straight-forward enough. If you are bringing your own **car**, you will need a valid national driving licence, registration document and continental insurance cover. The most frequent cross-channel services operate from Dover (to Calais, Dunkerque and Boulogne). Other options include the Channel Tunnel and Ramsgate-Ostend. Possibly the best option is to cross from Harwich to Hook of Holland with Stena Line's fast ferry for the drive through Holland and northern Germany. Eurolines operates long-distance **coaches** to Berlin from the UK and other European countries. Arrival in Berlin is at the central coach station Am Funkturm on Messedamm.

Berlin's new status as Germany's capital has now brought big investments in rail links to the city: new Inter City Express (ICE) **trains** now reach Berlin in 1hr 37min from Hanover and 4hr 10min from Frankfurt am Main, where there are con-nections from much of western Europe.

Berlin at a Glance

Berlin has an excellent network of **S-Bahn** (suburban) and **U-Bahn** (underground) lines that is constantly being expanded to ease inner-city travelling and reach further into the suburbs. The S-Bahn (denoted by a white 'S' on a green circle) and U-Bahn (a white 'U' on a blue square) **trains** run from about 05:00–00:30. On Friday and Saturday nights trains operate round the clock on most of the S-Bahn and U-Bahn network; trains run throughout at frequent intervals.

Double-decker **buses** operate throughout the city, but **trams** run only in the eastern part – rare foresight on the part of the former East Berlin's communist administration. The tram lines were ripped out of western Berlin back in the 1960s and the authorized vandalism is now regretted; moves are afoot to put trams back on western streets. Berlin's **night-bus** network is extensive; buses run half-hourly on designated night routes from 01:00–04:00 and are good for getting back to the hotel after a late night out on the town.

Tickets for Berlin's comprehensive transport system, operated by the **Berliner Verkehrs-Betriebe (BVG)**, are valid on trains, buses and trams. Single tickets are valid for two hours and you can

interrupt your journey as many times as you like. Short-distance tickets are valid for three stops on the train or for one bus or tram line. For one-day, seven-day or monthly tickets you buy a ticket for zones A and B, B and C or all three from a station ticket machine – they cannot be bought on the bus or tram. For a single bus or tram journey you pay the driver. The **Berlin WelcomeCard**, valid for two or three days, allows one adult and up to three children under 14 to travel on the BVG network at no extra cost and gives reductions of up to 50 per cent off a long list of attractions – including city sightseeing tours, boat trips, museums and theatres.

The metered beige Berlin **taxis** can be flagged down in the street – they are for hire if their yellow taxi sign is lit up. There are cab stands all over the city. All the leading international **car hire** companies are represented in Berlin. You can hire a car either from the airport on arrival, or at the companies' offices in the city centre. If you are driving yourself around Berlin, beware the weekday rush hours from 07:00–09:00 and 16:00–18:00. Parking ticket machines operate in the inner city area. The BVG transport network also includes **ferry** services in the Wannsee and Köpenick areas.

Before selecting your hotel, decide whether you want to stay in the western or eastern part of the city – that is, in the vicinity of the Ku'damm shopping and nightlife area, or close to the historical sights. In the west, there is a wider choice of all kinds of accommodation, from the simple **pensions** between the Ku'damm and Kantstraße to five-star grandeur around the Tiergarten – the legacy of pre-unification days. Nevertheless, since 1989 there has been considerable hotel investment in the former East Berlin and many international **hotel chains** are now represented in that part of the city. The **Berlin Tourismus** hotline, +49 (0) 30 25 00 25, can be used to book your accommodation – from a room in a luxury hotel to a bed in a **youth hostel** – before you leave home or on arrival in Berlin. The line is open Monday–Friday 08:00–19:00, Saturday–Sunday and public holidays 09:00–18:00. The fax number is +49 (0) 30 25 00 24 24. If you are telephoning the hotel direct from outside Berlin, the city code for all the properties listed is (030).

Eastern City
LUXURY
Adlon Kempinski, Unter den Linden 77, 10117 Berlin-Mitte, tel: 22 61 0, fax: 22 61

22 22. This hotel was opened in 1997 near the Brandenburg Gate on the site of the original Adlon, which was built in 1907 and then destroyed in World War II. With its 337 rooms, the Adlon is the last word in luxury.

Hilton, Mohrenstraße 30, 10117 Berlin-Mitte, tel: 20 23 0, fax: 20 23 42 69. Right on Gendarmenmarkt, the 354-room Hilton opened in 1991. Hilton was one of the first international chains to expand into Berlin after the collapse of the Wall.

Maritim ProArte, Friedrichstraße 151, 10117 Berlin-Mitte, tel: 20 33 5, fax: 20 33 40 90. The German hotel chain's property has 403 rooms and is situated just two minutes' walk from the Friedrichstraße rail station.

Radisson SAS, Karl-Liebknecht Straße 3, 10178 Berlin-Mitte, tel: 23 82 8, fax: 23 82 81 0. On the bank of the Spree, it has 427 rooms and suites. Some rooms look on to the AquaDom aquarium that rises from the hotel lobby; there is a 'Splash' leisure area.

Regent Berlin, Charlottenstraße 49, 10117 Berlin-Mitte, tel: 20 33 8, fax: 20 33 61 19. This is an excellent five-star hotel with 195 rooms, including 39 suites and an outstanding

reputation. It is situated close to the Gendarmenmarkt.

Westin Grand, Friedrichstraße 158–164, 10117 Berlin-Mitte, tel: 20 27 0, fax: 20 27 33 62. The Westin Grand opened its doors in 1987 and, during the two years before the Wall came down, established itself as East Berlin's best hotel. Still elegant, the 359-room hotel is part of the Westin chain.

Mid-range

Albrechtshof, Albrectstraße 8, 10117 Berlin-Mitte, tel: 308 86 0, fax: 308 86 100. Superior three-star hotel in quiet location close to Friedrichstraße.

Allegra, Albrechtstraße 17, 10117 Berlin-Mitte, tel: 308 86 0, fax: 308 86 100. This modern 79-room hotel is housed in a 145-year-old building and situated close to the theatre district.

Amelie, Reinhardstraße 21, 10117 Berlin-Mitte, tel: 28 04 05 08, fax: 28 04 05 09. Well-appointed mid-range hotel close to the theatre district and Friedrichstraße.

Ibis Berlin Mitte, Prenzlauer Allee 4, 10405 Berlin-Prenzlauer Berg, tel: 443 330, fax: 443 331 11. Typical modern Ibis hotel with 198 rooms, situated just a short tram ride away from the main city sights.

Kastanienhof, Kastanienallee 65, 10119 Berlin-Mitte, tel:

443 05 0, fax; 443 05 111. The Kastanienhof is a smart 35-room hotel-pension. It is conveniently situated between the city centre and Prenzlauer Berg.

Park Inn, Alexanderplatz 7, 10178 Berlin-Mitte, tel: 23 89 0, fax: 23 89 43 05. With its 1012 rooms on 30 floors, the former Forum Hotel is Berlin's largest hotel by far. The views over the city are excellent.

Budget

Aacron, Friedrichstraße 124, 10117 Berlin-Mitte, tel: 282 93 52, fax: 280 80 57. The Aacron is a comfortable 21-room 'discount hotel'.

Artist Hotel-Pension Die Loge, Friedrichstraße 115, 10117 Berlin-Mitte, tel/fax: 280 75 13. Cosy pension with just seven rooms.

Fabrik-Hostel Kreuzberg, Schlesische Straße 18, 10997 Berlin-Kreuzberg, tel: 611 82 54, fax: 618 29 74. Inexpensive accommodation in east Kreuzberg.

Juncker's Hotel Garni, Grünberger Straße 21, 10243 Berlin-Friedrichshain, tel: 29 33 55 0, fax: 29 33 55 55. Tastefully furnished 30-room budget hotel just east of the city centre.

Transit, Hagelberger Straße 53–54, 10965 Berlin-Kreuzberg, tel: 789 047 0, fax: 789 047 77. Popular west Kreuzberg budget hotel.

Berlin at a Glance

Western City

LUXURY

Crowne Plaza Berlin City-Center, Nürnberger Straße 65, 10787 Berlin-Schöneberg, tel: 21 00 70, fax: 213 20 09. This Holiday Inn hotel is situated near Berlin's big shops – KaDeWe *et al*. Beer drinkers in particular will enjoy the 423-room hotel's Pinte pub.

Grand Hyatt Berlin, Marlene-Dietrich-Platz 2, 10785 Berlin-Tiergarten, tel: 25 53 12 34, fax: 25 53 12 35. Post-unification five-star hotel, with 342 rooms. Handy for corporate executives doing business around high-rise Potsdamer Platz, but leisure guests may feel the ultra-modern surroundings lack a true Berlin identity.

InterContinental, Budapester Straße 2, 10787 Berlin-Tiergarten, tel: 26 02 0, fax: 26 02 26 00. Berlin's largest five-star hotel – it has 530 rooms and 54 suites – with the city's largest ballroom. It is especially popular with business guests.

Kempinski Bristol Berlin, Kurfürstendamm 27, 10719 Berlin-Charlottenburg, tel: 884 34 0, fax: 883 60 75. Opened in 1952, 'The Bristol' with its 301 rooms thrives on its fashionable Ku'damm address.

Palace, Im Europa-Center, 10789 Berlin-Charlottenburg, tel: 25 02 0, fax: 25 02 11 19. The Palace is situated oppo-site the zoo and next door to the Europa-Center indoor shopping complex; guests at the 282-room hotel may use the 800-sq-metre health spa facility.

Schloßhotel Im Grunewald, Brahmsstraße 10, 14193 Berlin-Wilmersdorf, tel: 895 84 0, fax: 895 84 800. Built as a Grunewald mansion for the aristocracy in 1912, the 52-room hotel offers Berlin's top luxury, and some of Berlin's top prices. The inte-rior was designed by Karl Lagerfeld.

MID-RANGE

Alexander, Pariser Straße 37, 10707 Berlin-Charlottenburg, tel: 88 71 650, fax: 88 71 65 65. Nicely designed three-star, with custom-built furniture, just off the Ku'damm

Charlottenburger Hof, Stuttgarter Platz 14, 10627 Berlin-Charlottenburg, tel: 329 070, fax: 323 37 23. Tidy 45-room hotel opposite Charlottenburg station.

Hamburg Ringotel Berlin, Landgrafenstraße 4, 10787 Berlin-Tiergarten, tel: 264 77 0, fax: 262 93 94. This well-priced 240-room hotel is convenient for KaDeWe and other large shops.

Ibis Berlin Messe, Messedamm 10, 14057 Berlin-Charlottenburg, tel: 303 930, fax: 301 95 36. A 191-room chain hotel, handy for the ICC conference centre.

Kanthotel, Kantstraße 111, 10627 Berlin-Charlottenburg, tel: 323 02 0, fax: 324 09 52. This newly extended 70-room hotel is a member of the Best Western chain.

Savoy, Fasanenstraße 9–10, 10623 Berlin-Charlottenburg, tel: 311 03 0, fax: 311 03 333. This is a good quality, 125-room hotel in the mid-priced range.

Zoo Berlin, Kurfürstendamm 25, 10719 Berlin-Charlottenburg, tel: 884 37 0, fax: 884 37 714. Right on the Ku'damm, this hotel's 136 rooms provide welcome rest for visiting shopaholics.

BUDGET

Alexandra Hotel-Pension, Wielandstraße 32, 10629 Berlin-Charlottenburg, tel: 881 21 07, fax: 88 57 78 18. Delightful rooms in a great location.

Haus der Begegnung, Landhausstraße 10, 10717 Berlin-Wilmersdorf, tel: 860 09 80, fax: 861 17 58. Well-priced hotel two U-Bahn stops south of the Ku'damm.

Hotel-Pension Charlottenburg, Grolmannstraße 32–33, 10623 Berlin-Charlottenburg, tel: 880 32 960, fax: 883 24 07. A simple and inexpensive establishment.

Pension Majesty, Mommsenstraße 55, 10629 Berlin-Charlottenburg, tel: 323 20 61, fax: 323 20 63. Cheap rooms between Kantstraße and the Ku'damm.

Pension Viola Nova,
Kantstraße 146, 10623 Berlin-Charlottenburg, tel: 315 72
60, fax: 312 33 14. Pension
providing excellent value for
money.

The variety of Berlin's **restaurants** is legendary – from **café**
or **bistro** simplicity to palatial
opulence, from traditional
1920s style to ultra-modern.
Hundreds of restaurants serve
the hearty fare for which
Germany is famous; alongside them are French, Italian,
Spanish, Turkish, Asian,
Caribbean, Mexican and a
host of **other nationalities.**

The latest fashionable
area for dining out in Berlin is
Prenzlauer Berg, the former
working-class district just
outside the centre, where
countless restaurants and bars
have opened in recent years.
In **Kreuzberg**, too, there is
plenty of scope to eat well
and cheaply close to the city
centre, while **Schöneberg** is
also making its mark on the
restaurant scene. By far the
widest choice of places to eat
is to be found in **Charlottenburg**, west of the Tiergarten
between the radiating
Ku'damm and Kantstraße. In
the eastern section of the city,
character restaurants have
been incorporated into the
restored **Nikolaiviertel**, while
just north of the city centre
Oranienburger Straße is the
new place to head for.

Eastern City
LUXURY
Französischer Hof,
Jägerstraße 56, Mitte,
tel: 20 17 71 70. Art
Nouveau splendour on
the Gendarmenmarkt; the
cuisine is German-French.
Vau, Jägerstraße 54–55,
Mitte, tel: 202 97 30.
Leading chef Kolja Kleeberg
has further enhanced what
has become one of Berlin's
leading gourmet addresses.
Zur Gerichtslaube, Poststraße
28, Mitte, tel: 241 56 97.
Enjoy typical Berlin fare
beneath the vaulted ceiling
of the Nikolaiviertel's rebuilt
former courthouse, dating
from 1270.

MID-RANGE
Borchardt, Französische
Straße 47, Mitte, tel: 20 39
71 17. Classic restaurant by
Gendarmenmarkt, serving
modern French and Italian
cuisine.
Café Oren, Oranienburger
Straße 28, Mitte, tel: 282
82 28. Top Jewish and
Arab fare close to the
New Synagogue.
Fernsehturm Telecafé,
Alexanderplatz, Mitte, tel:
242 33 33. The restaurant in
the TV tower, 207m (680ft)
above Berlin, offers great
views and an excellent meal
selection.
Jedermans's, Unter den
Linden 12, Mitte, tel: 206 04
980. Excellent light lunches at
a reasonable price.

Opernpalais, Unter den
Linden 5, Mitte, tel: 20 26 83.
Here you can choose from the
Operncafé (breakfast
buffet/patisserie), Königin Luise
(gourmet) and Operntreff, a
Parisian-style café.
Reinhard's, Poststraße 28,
Mitte, tel: 242 52 95.
Effectively recreates the
refined atmosphere of
1920s Berlin in the old
Nikolaiviertel.
Sophieneck, Grosse Hamburger Straße 37, Mitte, tel:
28 34 065. Good home cooking in a cosy atmosphere.
Zum Nussbaum, Am Nussbaum 3, Mitte, tel: 242 30 95.
A recreated 16th-century
Nikolaiviertel restaurant
bombed out of existence in
World War II. Touristy but
deservedly popular.
Zur Letzten Instanz,
Waisenstraße 14–16, Mitte,
tel: 242 55 28. Artists and
celebrities frequent Berlin's
oldest restaurant in a pub just
south of Alexanderplatz.

BUDGET
Café Adler, Friedrichstraße
206, Kreuzberg, tel: 251 89
65. Next to the former
Checkpoint Charlie, it was the
last building in West Berlin in
its former life as a pharmacy.
Weihenstephaner, Neue
Promenade 5, Mitte, tel:
25 76 28 71. Well-priced
Bavarian fare at Hackescher
Markt washed down by beer
from Germany's oldest
brewery, Weihenstephaner.

Berlin at a Glance

Western City
LUXURY
Alt Luxemburg,
Windscheidstraße 31,
Charlottenburg, tel: 323 87
30. Enjoy cuisine with a
French accent in the refined
atmosphere of one of Berlin's
top restaurants.
Ana E Bruno, Sophie-
Charlotten-Straße 101,
Charlottenburg, tel: 325 71
10. Classic Italian restaurant
with warm and informal
atmosphere.
Bamberger Reiter,
Regensburger Straße 7,
Schöneberg, tel: 218 42 82.
Reservations are advised for
this farmhouse-style venue
with one of Berlin's top
reputations.
**Dachgarten Restaurant
Käfer am Bundestag,**
The Reichstag, Tiergarten,
tel: 22 62 99 33. Dine at the
top of the Reichstag building
looking on to Sir Norman
Foster's dome.

MID-RANGE
Arche Noah, Fasanenstraße
79–80, Charlottenburg,
tel: 882 61 38. Widely
acclaimed kosher restaurant
in the Jüdisches Gemeindehaus (Jewish Community
Centre).
Café Bleibtreu,
Bleibtreustraße 45,
Charlottenburg, tel: 881 47
56. Highly popular and a
personal favourite. Bags of
atmosphere, wide German
menu. The typical Berlin

breakfast buffet, served from
09:30–15:30 weekends and
holidays, is a speciality.
Café Kranzler, Kurfürstendamm 18, Charlottenburg,
tel: 887 183 925. Berlin's
best-known coffee and cake
house, it was formerly
situated on Unter den Linden.
A tourist hot spot, but the
terrace is good people-
watching territory.
Cassambalis, Grolmanstraße
35, Charlottenburg, tel: 885
47 47. Mediterranean-style
restaurant with a wide menu
and a delightfully relaxed
atmosphere.
Don Quijote, Bleibtreustraße
41, Charlottenburg, tel: 881
32 08. Friendly and authentic
Spanish with good atmos-
phere and wide menu.
Florian, Grolmannstraße 52,
Charlottenburg, tel: 313 91
84. Popular with the literati
for its Bavarian cuisine.
Laternchen, Windscheidstraße 24, Charlottenburg,
tel: 324 68 82. Traditional
Berlin-style cooking at reasonable prices.
La Piazza, Savignyplatz 13,
Charlottenburg, tel: 312 39
90. Relaxed Greek-Italian
with outdoor dining on leafy
Savignyplatz in summer.
Mar Y Sol, Savignyplatz 5,
Charlottenburg, tel: 313 25
93. Spanish restaurant with
great tapas selection. Dine
on the leafy terrace looking
on to the fashionable Berlin
square.
Storch, Wartburgstraße 54,

Schöneberg, tel: 784 20 59.
Berlin's leading Alsatian
restaurant, Storch is just a
few minutes walk from
Schöneberg Town Hall.

BUDGET
Luisen-Bräu, Luisenplatz 1,
Charlottenburg, tel: 341 93
88. A cheap and highly
cheerful restaurant – good
plain food washed down with
home-brewed beer. Near
Schloß Charlottenburg.

Prenzlauer Berg
Bangin, Kollwitzstraße 56,
Prenzlauer Berg, tel: 40 05 68
30. A culinary trip around the
world with good vegetarian
choice. Lots of outside tables
in summer.
Istoria, Kollwitzstraße 64,
Prenzlauer Berg, tel: 44 05 02
08. Pasta, pizzas, weekend
brunch buffet, situated just off
Kollwitzplatz.
Pasternak, Knaackstraße
22–24, Prenzlauer Berg, tel:
441 33 99. Well-rated
Russian speciality restaurant.
Restauration 1900,
Husemannstraße 1,
Prenzlauer Berg, tel: 442 24
94. Acclaimed bistro-style
eating and drinking house
on the north side of
Kollwitzplatz.

Kreuzberg
Altes Zollhaus, Carl-Herz-
Ufer 30, Kreuzberg, tel: 692
33 00. Restored customs
house by the Landwehrkanal
in north Kreuzberg serving

Berlin at a Glance

mid-priced German fare. Attractive summer garden.

Austria, Bergmannstraße 30, Kreuzberg, tel: 694 44 40. Enjoy Viennese coffee specialities and wholesome Austrian cooking in rustic surroundings.

Hostaria del Monte Croce, Mittenwalderstraße 6, Kreuzberg, tel: 694 39 68. Good Italian eatery in west Kreuzberg. The restaurant has its own courtyard.

ENTERTAINMENT

Bars and Pubs

If a beer beckons after a long day's museum bashing, look for a sign saying 'Kneipe' – it means 'pub'. There are hundreds, if not thousands, in Berlin, so it won't take you too long to find one. Many Berlin bars also serve light meals and most keep extremely sociable hours – closing time is generally reckoned to be any time between midnight and 04:00.

Bar am Lützowplatz, Lützowplatz, Schöneberg, tel: 262 68 07. One of Berlin's longest and narrowest bars, it has a portrait of Mao Tse-tung as a focal point.

Broker's Bier Börse, Schiffbauer Damm 8, Mitte, tel: 30 87 22 93. Customers determine the prices for 16 draught beers in this stock exchange theme pub – the greater the demand, the higher the price (and vice versa). Good food, too.

Felsenkeller, Akazienstraße 2, Schöneberg, tel: 781 34 47. This is an established bar which now attracts a much younger clientele.

Irish Harp Pub, Giesebrechtstraße 15, Charlottenburg, tel: 22 32 87 35. This pub is full of traditional Irish cheer, often with live music. More Guinness at the Irish Bar in the Europa-Center and the Kilkenny at Hackescher Markt S-Bahn station.

Leydicke, Mansteinstraße 4, Schöneberg, tel: 216 29 73. Old-style drinking establishment worth visiting for the traditional ambience alone. It has been run by the same family for over a century.

Mutter Hoppe, Rathausstraße 21, Mitte, tel: 241 56 25. Old-fashioned Nikolaiviertel pub serving hearty food. Songs from the 1920s and 1930s on Friday and Saturday evenings.

Robbengatter, Grunewaldstraße 55, Schöneberg, tel: 853 52 55. Pool bar offering good food and drink.

Zur Weissen Maus, Ludwigkirchplatz 12, Charlottenburg, tel: 88 67 92 88. Big-city atmosphere in this cocktail bar playing music from the 1930s and 1940s.

Cabaret

Berlin's reputation for all-singing, all-dancing cabaret is legion, though nowadays the performances are more akin to variety shows aimed at international consumption. Visitors should take care not to confuse cabaret with Kabarett, the acerbic political satires for which rather more than a working knowledge of German is needed.

Bar Jeder Vernunft, Schaperstraße 24, Wilmersdorf, tel: 883 15 82. Adventurous theatre a few blocks south of the zoo; be prepared for the unexpected.

Chamäleon Varieté, Rosenthaler Straße 40–41 (Hackesche Höfe), Mitte, tel: 40 00 590. Traditional variety in the restored Hackesche Höfe: clowns, jugglers, acrobats and the like.

Chez Nous, Marburger Straße 14, Charlottenburg, tel: 213 18 10. Berlin folk are fond of their transvestite shows – this one is especially popular and therefore reservations are advised.

Friedrichstadtpalast, Friedrichstraße 107, Mitte, tel: 23 26 23 26. Europe's biggest revue theatre and the eastern city's best-known night spot. It is very popular with tour groups – book early.

Scheinbar Varieté, Monumentenstraße 9, Schöneberg, tel: 784 55 39. Twenties-style revues in Berlin's southern suburb.

Wintergarten Varieté, Potsdamer Straße 96,

Tiergarten, tel: 25 00 88 88. Top-quality entertainers make it a night out to remember – this venue offers a great mix of cabaret and variety. Dine before the show.

Nightlife
Berlin's night scene is an ever-changing collection of discos, music bars and the like. What is there one year may have gone the next; here are a few of the ever-presents.

Alte Kantine, Kulturbrauerei, Knaackstraße 97, Prenzlauer Berg, tel: 44 34 19 52. Wide range of sounds in a former brewery complex.

Big Eden, Kurfürstendamm 202, Charlottenburg, tel: 53 32 030. Popular Ku'damm spot with a large dance floor and elaborate light show. Attracts a wide clientele.

Matrix Berlin, Warschauer Platz 18, Friedrichshain, tel: 293 69 990. Lively club with dancing on four floors and the latest in lighting technology.

Oxymoron, Rosenthaler Straße 40–41 (Hackescher Höfe), Mitte, tel: 28 39 18 86. This popular nightspot in Hof 1 recaptures 1920s flair with its stylish bar.

Quasimodo, Kantstraße 12a, Charlottenburg, tel: 312 80 86. Long-established venue for live jazz, funk, blues and soul. It is usually packed, so get there early.

SHOPPING
Berlin takes quite some beating for the quality of its shopping. Tourists generally make a leisurely stroll down **Kurfürstendamm** a priority, if only to window-gaze at the vast array of quality goods for sale in the shops. But nowadays the city's number one shopping street is facing some tough competition from other parts of the city – mainly from the fast-evolving **Friedrichstraße**, but also from the Arkaden gallery at Potsdamer Platz. And those visitors who prefer to avoid the shopping crowds will still be able to find an excellent selection of stylish individual shops in the **Hackesche Höfe** area of the city.

Berlin's shopping mecca is **KaDeWe** (which is short for Kaufhaus des Westens), Europe's largest department store that appears to sell just about everything you can imagine. The food floor is a particular treat. Right across Tauentzienstraße is the **Europa-Center**, an indoor shopping complex on two floors enhanced by its watery centrepiece complete with hanging greenery. Close by is the start of the Ku'damm, crammed with **department stores**, **high-fashion shops** and **boutiques** – along with several cinemas and a good few restaurants in which to recover from the activity of the buying spree.

Off the Ku'damm, situated along side streets such as Fasanenstraße and Bleibtreustraße, are the most expensive **fashion houses**: big names in the area include Jil Sander, René Lezard, Karl Lagerfeld, Yves Saint Laurent and Louis Vuitton. Here, too, are top **jewellers** Cartier and Tiffany. Also on the Ku'damm is a Meissen shop selling the expensive German **porcelain** (there is another on Unter den Linden).

At Knesebeckstraße 33 in Charlottenburg, the Marga Schöller bookshop has a wide assortment of English-language books and film literature.

While Unter den Linden offers relatively few retail outlets in the eastern city, nearby Friedrichstraße is currently being developed as the shopping hub of the eastern city. To the south of Unter den Linden is **Galeries Lafayette**, while **Quartier 206**, with its boutiques and designer outlets, is also well worth visiting.

Situated at the heart of the Potsdamer Platz development, the twin-level shopping arcade offers all kinds of shops – a contrast to the cluster of gift shops that adorn the revived Nikolaiviertel. In and around the Hackesche Höfe, on Oranienburger Straße, Rosenthaler Straße, Auguststraße, Sophienstraße and Gipsstraße are more

Berlin at a Glance

unusual fashion and designer shops. Among the city's most popular **souvenirs** are the ubiquitous Berlin bear and models of the Brandenburg Gate. At last there are no longer pieces of the Berlin Wall – it was quite amazing how long pieces of the Wall survived.

If you are in Berlin in late November or December, take in the **Christmas markets** with their many colourful stalls – and sample the mulled wine called Glühwein. The two principal Christmas markets are by the Kaiser Wilhelm Memorial Church at the end of the Ku'damm and on Alexanderplatz. They open from late morning until 21:00 or 22:00.

TOURS AND EXCURSIONS

Berlin's rather wide streets make the city ideal for sightseeing from the comfort of a twin-deck **excursion bus**, and full-day and half-day tours operate daily. The classic hop-on, hop-off City-Circle sightseeing tour with commentary in eight languages operates from April to October with a number of operators, among them Berolina, BBS and Berliner City Tour. The complete trip takes two hours, but half-hourly departures allow you to jump off and re-board at 15 stops around the city; your ticket is valid for a day.

A similar Top-Tour-Berlin offer from the local transport authority BVG makes 16 stops along the way between the Ku'damm and Alexanderplatz.

Cheaper by far is the 100 regular **bus** service, which runs from the Zoo station right through the middle of Berlin to Alexanderplatz. A standard single ticket allows you two hours to get off as many times as you like while heading in the same direction. Full-day trips operate to Dresden and Meissen, and also to Spreewald, including a punting trip. There are half-day excursions to Potsdam/Sanssouci and trips out to the Berlin lakes.

For many, however, the best way to see Berlin is **on foot**, and Insider Tour (tel: 692 31 49) offers a selection of guided walks year-round, including the Famous Insider Walk Tour taking four hours. Meeting points are the Zoo station and Hackescher Markt station. **BBS Berliner Bären Stadtrundfahrt**, Seeburger Straße 19b, 13581 Berlin-Spandau, tel: 35 19 52 70.
Berliner City Tour, Budapester Straße 16A, 10787 Berlin-Tiergarten, tel: 257 987 62.
Berolina, Meinekestraße 3, 10719 Berlin-Charlottenburg, tel: 88 56 80 30.
BVB Bus-Verkehr-Berlin, Grenzallee 15, 12057 Berlin-

Neukölln, tel: 68 38 91 0.
Top-Tour-Berlin, BVG Stadttouristik, tel: 256 255 69.

A number of companies operate **boat trips** in and around Berlin – there are trips on the Spree and the Landwehrkanal, and you can also go further afield between Spandau, Wannsee and Potsdam. Contact one of these:
Reederei Bruno Winkler, Mierendorffstraße 16, 10589 Berlin-Charlottenburg, tel: 349 95 95.
Stern und Kreis, Puschkinallee 16–17, 12435 Berlin-Treptow, tel: 536 36 00.

USEFUL CONTACTS

Half-price tickets for theatre, cabaret and concert performances, tel: 230 99 30.
Airports – information line (within Germany), tel: 0 18 05 00 01 86.
ADAC – German Automobile Club, tel: 0 18 05 10 11 12.
Breakdown service, tel: 0 18 02 22 22 22.
Train information, tel: 0 18 05 19 41 95.
BVG (local transport authority) timetable and ticket inquiries, tel: 1 94 49.
BVG lost property office, Potsdamer Straße 180/182, 10783 Berlin-Schöneberg, tel: 1 94 49. Open Monday–Thursday 09:00–18:00, Friday 09:00–14:00.
Taxis, tel: 6 90 22, 26 10 26, 21 01 01, 21 02 02, 881 15 46.

Travel Tips

Tourist information

The **German National Tourist Office** is represented in the United Kingdom (London), the USA (New York), Canada (Toronto), Japan (Tokyo) and also throughout Europe. The marketing of Berlin is carried out by **Berlin Tourismus Marketing**, Am Karlsbad 11, 10785 Berlin, tel: +49 (30) 25 00 25, fax: +49 (30) 25 00 24 24. There are four Berlin Infostores:

Hauptbahnhof, (main station), Europa Platz Entrance (daily 08:00–22:00).

Neues Kranzler Eck, at Kurfürstendamm 21 (Mon–Thur 09:30–20:00, Fri–Sat 09:30–21:00, Sun 09:30–18:00).

Brandenburg Gate, (Apr–Oct daily 09:30–18:00, Nov–Mar daily 10:00–18:00).

Reichstag, Berlin Pavilion (Apr–Oct daily 08:30–20:00, Nov–March daily 10:00–18:00).

A **Mobility Service**, offering advice for disabled people, is offered by Mobidat on tel: 74 77 71 15. It has a database with information on accessibility to public facilities.

Embassies and Consulates:

American Embassy, Neustädtische Kirchstraße 4–5, 10117 Berlin, tel: 830 50.

Australian Embassy, Wallstraße 76–79, 10179 Berlin, tel: 88 00 880, fax: 88 00 88 210.

British Embassy, Wilhelmstraße 70–71, 10117 Berlin, tel: 204 570, fax: 2045 7594.

Canadian Embassy, Leipziger Platz 17, 10117, Berlin, tel: 203 120, fax: 2031 2121.

Irish Embassy, Friedrichstraße 200, 10117 Berlin, tel: 220 720, fax: 22 07 22 99.

South African Embassy, Tiergartenstraße 18, 10785 Berlin, tel: 220 730, fax: 22 07 31 90.

Entry Requirements

British nationals need a valid passport to enter Germany. Other EU nationals can enter on production of a National Identity Card. Nationals of Australia, Canada, New Zealand and the United States do not need a visa for stays of up to three months.

Customs

The duty-free allowance for goods imported into Germany is: one litre of spirits or two litres of fortified wine, plus two litres of wine, 200 cigarettes (or 50 cigars or 250g tobacco) and 50g perfume. When duty is paid within the EU, the alcohol/tobacco volume is 10 litres of spirits, 20 litres of fortified wine, 90 litres of wine and 110 litres of beer; plus 3200 cigarettes (or 400 cigarillos, 200 cigars or 3kg tobacco).

Health Requirements

No vaccinations are necessary to enter Germany. Free or reduced-cost emergency health treatment is available to British visitors on production of a European Health Insurance Card, which has replaced the Form E111 in the UK. All visitors are advised to arrange their own comprehensive travel and medical insurance. Keep receipts and invoices – you will need them when making a claim. (For emergency telephone numbers, *see* Health Services on page 126.)

Getting There

By air: This is the easiest way to get there. Berlin is served by direct flights from 70 countries and there are many more routes involving a change of aircraft elsewhere in Germany. British Airways flies from London Heathrow to Berlin's Tegel airport and Germany's national airline, Lufthansa, offers connections through Frankfurt/Main and other German cities. Low-cost airlines fly from UK airports. The former East Berlin airport of Schönefeld is being developed to become Berlin-Brandenburg International; by 2011 it will handle all Berlin flights and Tegel airport will close. In the meantime, international flights use Schönefeld, 20km (12 miles) southeast of the city centre, and Tegel, 8km (5 miles) north of the central area. Schönefeld has its own Airport Express train into the city centre. It operates half-hourly with the same single fare as the U-Bahn and S-Bahn rail networks. Travellers arriving at Tegel have bus links to two U-Bahn (underground) stations: Jakob-Kaiser-Platz (western city)and Kurt-Schuhmacher-Platz (eastern city).

By road: There are excellent motorway connections across Europe on to the Berliner Ring, the Autobahn that surrounds Berlin and provides access to all parts of the city. To drive in Germany, or to hire a car, you need a valid national driving licence. Visitors from Canada, the USA, Australia, New Zealand and South Africa need an international driving

licence. Drivers must have green card insurance cover, though this is not compulsory for EU citizens; motoring insurers are increasingly building European cover into their domestic policies, so it pays to shop around. You must also carry the car's registration papers and the red warning triangle compulsory in most European countries. In Germany you drive on the right; drivers must be 18 or older. Seat belts must be worn in the front and back of the car, and children under 12 may not travel in the front seats.

USEFUL PHRASES

English • *German*
Do you speak English? •
Sprechen Sie Englisch?
Excuse me • *Entschuldigung*
Goodbye/Bye •
Auf Wiedersehen/Tschüss
Good day • *Guten Tag*
Good evening • *Guten Abend*
Good morning •
Guten Morgen
How much is that? •
Wieviel kostet es?
I (don't) understand •
Ich verstehe (nicht)
How/When/Where? •
Wie/Wann/Wo?
Please/Thank you (very much)
• *Bitte/Danke (schön)*
Write it down, please •
Bitte Schreiben Sie es auf
Yes/No • *Ja/Nein*
airport • *der Flughafen*
bill/check • *die Rechnung*
bus • *der Bus*
car • *das Auto*
castle • *das Schloß*
cathedral • *der Dom*
church • *die Kirche*
closed • *geschlossen*

Customs • *Zoll*
departure • *Abfahrt*
entrance • *Eingang/Einfahrt*
exit/emergency exit •
Ausgang/Notausgang
gents • *Herren*
hospital • *der Krankenhaus*
identification • *Ausweis*
ladies • *Damen*
lake • *der See*
menu • *die Speisekarte*
occupied • *besetzt*
open • *offen*
passport • *der Pass*
petrol • *das Benzin*
pharmacy • *die Apotheke*
police • *die Polizei*
post office • *das Postamt*
railway station • *der Bahnhof*
river • *der Fluss*
stamp • *die Briefmarke*
street • *die Straße*
ticket • *die Fahrkarte*
timetable • *der Fahrplan*
today • *heute*
tomorrow • *morgen*
train • *der Zug*
tram • *die Strassenbahn*
yesterday • *gestern*

Kneipe - pub

By train: The international train bringing you to Berlin deposits you at the impressive new Berlin Hauptbahnhof, formerly Lehrte Stadtbahnhof, across the River Spree from the Reichstag building and the Spreebogen area of new government buildings. As a key part of city-centre redevelopment, the former S-Bahn station has been turned into a new superstation of glass and steel – it is the largest rail hub in Europe and has taken over the roles of the Zoological Gardens and Ostbahnhof (formerly Hauptbahnhof) stations, still serving the western and eastern parts of the city respectively. Ongoing investment in Germany's rail network means Berlin can now be reached by the sleek silver-grey ICE (Inter City Express) trains in 1hr 37min from Hanover and a little over 4hrs from Frankfurt am Main.

What to Pack

In **winter**, take your warmest clothing. If it is cold in the west of the city, it will feel bitingly so east of the Tiergarten, with icy winds sweeping in from the Baltic across the city's open squares. Pack your thickest coat, your fur-lined boots and a hat. In **spring** and **autumn**, too, it pays to be sensibly kitted out. Though it is warm when the sun shines, the air cools quickly and evenings can be cold. For **summer**, take light or medium-weight clothing – T-shirt, shorts and swimwear for a lakeside picnic. Though summer in Berlin is rarely excessively hot, sightseeing can be tiring and it is advisable to have a supply of cool cotton clothing. It is worth taking rainwear at any time as Berlin's rainfall occurs year-round. Or pack a fold-up umbrella – it will do the job just as well.

Money Matters

Currency: Germany was one of the first EU countries to embrace the Euro in January 1999. ATMs are widespread.

Credit Cards: Visa, American Express, EuroCard, Diners Club and MasterCard are widely accepted in hotels, shops and restaurants. However, some businesses in the east of the city will accept only cash. There is a 16 per cent VAT levy on goods and services.

Currency exchange: Change money and travellers' cheques at bureaux and banks – look for the Wechsel (exchange) sign. Hotels and some travel agencies will exchange money, but at less favourable rates. Bureaux include **American Express**, Bayreuther Straße 37, 10787 Berlin-Schöneberg, tel: 21 47 62 92; also Friedrichstraße 172, 10117 Berlin-Mitte, tel: 20 17 400; **Thomas Cook**, Friedrichstraße 56, 10117

Berlin-Mitte, tel: 20 16 59 16.

Tipping in restaurants is at your discretion. The bill usually includes a service charge, but it is customary to round up the amount by 5–10 per cent.

Accommodation

Visitors will find all types of accommodation – from youth hostels and guesthouses to mid-range hotels and the ultimate in five-star luxury. Berlin Tourismus Marketing gives a complete A to Z of accommodation in the city. Accommodation can be booked in advance on the BTM Hotline, tel: +49 (30) 25 00 25, fax: +49 (30) 25 00 24 24. The service operates Monday–Friday 08:00–19:00, Saturday–Sunday and public holidays 09:00–18:00.

Eating Out

Berlin is superbly served by top-quality eating houses – restaurants of every culinary persuasion that range from budget to Michelin-rated. Many open at around 09:30 to serve breakfast – and are still serving it in mid-afternoon. You simply choose English, French, Belgian, German or whatever and tuck in. Hundreds of restaurants serve German fare and hundreds more tempt you with anything from Turkish to Caribbean. They tend to remain open late, often until 01:00 or 02:00. For a quick midday bite, *Imbiss* stands all over the city serve snacks that vary from the ubiquitous burger or filled jacket potato to a plastic bowl piled with Chinese noodles.

CONVERSION CHART		
From	**To**	**Multiply By**
Millimetres	Inches	0.0394
Metres	Yards	1.0936
Metres	Feet	3.281
Kilometres	Miles	0.6214
Square kilometres	Square miles	0.386
Hectares	Acres	2.471
Litres	Pints	1.760
Kilograms	Pounds	2.205
Tonnes	Tons	0.984
To convert Celsius to Fahrenheit: x 9 ÷ 5 + 32		

Transport

Berlin's extensive public transport system incorporates the S-Bahn (suburban) and U-Bahn (underground) railways, trams in the eastern part of the city, and buses. It is administered by the BVG (Berliner Verkehrs-Betriebe), which sells single, short-distance, one-day, seven-day and monthly tickets that cover the entire network. Buy your single rail ticket or multi-journey ticket from the large yellow or orange ticket machine at the station (instructions in English) and validate it in the small red machine on the platform – or at the bus stop. Buy your bus or tram ticket from the driver. For public transport information, tel: 1 94 49 for U-Bahn, bus, tram and ferry (24-hour service) and tel: 29 74 33 33 for S-Bahn (Mon–Fri 06:30–22:00, Sat–Sun 07:00–20:00).

Rail: There are 16 **S-Bahn** lines (stations have a white 'S' on a green circle outside). Trains run from around 05:00 until 00:30, with the S7 line (Schönefeld Airport-Westkreuz) operating round the clock at weekends. The nine **U-Bahn** lines operate similar hours, with trains on some lines operating every 15min throughout the night at weekends. The Airport Express train (RE4, RE5) runs between Schönefeld Airport and Zoologischer Garten half-hourly from 05:00 to 23:30 for the cost of a single U-Bahn or S-Bahn ticket.

Buses: Berlin was one of the first cities outside London to operate double-decker buses: seeing the city from the top deck is an obvious attraction. A popular route with tourists is No. 100, which heads east from Zoologischer Garten station, passing the Brandenburg Gate and most of the eastern city sights on its way to Alexanderplatz. Night buses replace the S-Bahn and U-Bahn on over 54 routes during the time trains are not running: 00:30–04:30. Bus stops are identified by a green 'H' within a yellow circle.

Trams: Berlin's tram network is a legacy from communist times; the 21 lines are all in the eastern part of the city and its outskirts. Modern yellow trams have replaced the old ones that trundled through the streets of the former East Berlin, and there are plans to extend the network into the west of the city. A good starting point for a tram ride through eastern Berlin is Hackescher Markt, by the S-Bahn station, from where routes radiate towards the distant suburbs.

Car hire: With such a good public transport system, it is seldom necessary to hire a car. If you do need your own transport, hire from the rental desks in Tegel or Schönefeld airport and leave the car at the airport on your way home.

Taxis: There are stands for Berlin's beige-coloured taxis all over town – or you can flag down a cab in the street if its yellow taxi sign is lit up.

Velotaxi rickshaws ply many routes in summer – catch them at designated stops, tel: 0800 83 56 82 94.

Bicycles can be hired and, with Berlin's proliferation of cycle lanes, are a good way to get around. Fahrradstation has rental outlets with 2000 bikes for rent at Hackesche Höfe, Hof 7, tel: 28 38 48 48; at Auguststraße 29A, Mitte, tel: 28 59 96 61; Leipziger Straße 56, Mitte, tel: 66 64 91 80; and Bergmannstraße 9, Kreuzberg, tel: 215 1566.

Business Hours

Though there are no standard opening hours for shops, most open Monday–Friday 09:00–18:30, Saturday 09:00–14:00. They are closed on Saturday afternoon, all day Sunday and public holidays. Recent legislation allows shops to stay open until 20:00 on weekdays and 16:00 on Saturdays. Banking hours are generally Monday–Friday 08:30–13:00 and 14:00–16:00 (until 17:30 on Thursday); the banks do not open on Saturday or Sunday. Airport and railway station *bureaux de change* usually open from 06:00–22:00.

Time Difference

Berlin is on Central European Time, one hour ahead of GMT in winter and two hours

PUBLIC HOLIDAYS

1 January • New Year's Day
6 January • Epiphany
March/April • Good Friday and Easter Monday
1 May • Labour Day
May • Ascension Day
May/June • Whit Monday
3 October • Unity Day
1 November • All Saints Day
25 December • Christmas Day
26 December • Boxing Day

ahead of GMT in summer; the 24-hour clock is widely used.

Communications

International telephone calls can be made from public call boxes – dial the following international code first: United Kingdom 0044, Ireland 00353, Australia 0061, Canada and USA 001, New Zealand 0064, South Africa 0027 (don't forget to omit the '0' from the area code). Kiosks take coins and phone cards. Calls from hotels are generally much more expensive – it is far cheaper to dial abroad from a call box and ask the recipient to phone you back. Tell them to dial 0049 (for Germany), then 30 (for Berlin), followed by the number on the phone in front of you. Useful numbers: directory enquiries, tel: 11 833; international enquiries, tel: 11 834.

Electricity

The standard continental European 220 volts AC. Two-pin sockets – an adaptor is needed for British and American appliances.

Weights and Measures

Germany uses the metric system.

Health Services

Medical emergency service, tel: 31 00 31.
Poison emergency service, tel: 1 92 40.
Dental emergency, tel: 89 00 43 33
Drugs emergency service, tel: 1 92 37.
Pharmacy on call (information), tel: 0 11 89.

Personal Safety

Visitors in any city should guard against petty theft – and Berlin is no exception. Entrust your valuables to the hotel safe rather than leaving them in your room, and beware of pickpockets on crowded public transport and in busy shops. If you have a car, keep valuables out of sight and the vehicle locked and secured. Report any theft to your hotel and the police – if you make an insurance claim you will need a certificate from the police to show they were informed. Credit card insurance is wise: a phone call home in the event of loss can save you having to make international calls to companies. Carry photocopies of your passport, air ticket, driving licence and other documents when travelling – they can save no end of hassle later.

Emergencies

Police, tel: 110.
Fire Brigade, tel: 112.
Ambulance, tel: 112.
Gay and lesbian help is available at Mommsenstraße 45, Berlin-Charlottenburg, tel: 23 36 90 70 (Mon–Thu 09:00–20:00, Fri 09:00–18:00).
Gay and lesbian hotline, tel: 19446 216 3336.
Crisis helpline, tel: 0800 111 0111.
Medical, see Health Services.

Etiquette

It is polite to greet shopkeepers with Guten Tag (good day) and Auf Wiedersehen (goodbye) on entering and leaving their premises. In crowds, Entschuldigen Sie bitte (ex-cuse me please) can help you find a way through. Follow the locals' example and don't jump pedestrian lights – the traffic light sequence may catch you unawares and you may receive an on-the-spot fine.

Language

Pronunciation of German is not difficult (see page 23), so do learn a few phrases. Though English is widely understood in Berlin – increasingly so in view of the city's recently acquired capital status – you may find it is less so in the eastern part of the city. The locals, as everywhere, will appreciate visitors' efforts to converse in German.

GOOD READING

• **Bullock, Alan** (1954) Hitler: A Study in Tyranny, Penguin.
• **Childs, David** (1984) The GDR – Moscow's German Ally, Unwin Hyman.
• **Döblin, Alfred** (1929) Berlin Alexanderplatz, Penguin/Ungar.
• **Isherwood, Christopher** (1939) Goodbye to Berlin, Methuen/New Directions.
• **Reissner, Alexander** (1984) Berlin 1675–1945, Oswald Wolff.
• **Shirer, William L** (1960) The Rise and Fall of the Third Reich, Secker & Warburg.
• **Simmons, Michael** (1988) Berlin: The Dispossessed City, Hamish Hamilton.
• **Taylor, A J P** (1955) Bismarck: The Man and the Statesman, Hamish Hamilton.
• **Trevor-Roper, Hugh** (1947) The Last Days of Hitler, Macmillan.

INDEX

Note: Numbers in **bold** indicate photographs